PATRICIA CORNELIUS is a founding member of Melbourne Workers Theatre. She's a playwright, novelist and dramaturge. She's a recipient of a Fellowship from the Theatre Board of the Australia Council and the winner of 2010 NSW Premier's Literary Award, 2006 Patrick White Playwright's Award, 2009 Richard Wherrett Prize, 2003 Wal Cherry Award, The Jill Blewitt Award and the R.E. Ross Trust Award. Her plays have earned her eight AWGIES for stage, community, theatre for young people, and feature film adaptation. She has written over twenty-five plays. Her most recent works are *Savages*, *Slut*, *Love* and *The Call*.

*Pamela Rabe as Bowers in the 2010 fortyfivedownstairs production of
DO NOT GO GENTLE… in Melbourne. (Photo: Jeff Busby)*

DO NOT GO GENTLE

PATRICIA CORNELIUS

THE BERRY MAN

CURRENCY PLAYS

First published in 2011
by Currency Press Pty Ltd,
PO Box 2287, Strawberry Hills, NSW, 2012, Australia
enquiries@currency.com.au
www.currency.com.au

Copyright: Introduction © Julian Meyrick, 2011; *Do Not Go Gentle...* © Patricia Cornelius, 2010; Introduction © Susie Dee, 2011; *The Berry Man* © Patricia Cornelius, 2010.

Any performance or public reading of *Do Not Go Gentle...* or *The Berry Man* is forbidden unless a licence has been received from the author or the author's agent. The purchase of this book in no way gives the purchaser the right to perform the plays in public, whether by means of a staged production or a reading. All applications for public performance should be addressed to HLA Management, PO Box 1536, Strawberry Hills NSW 2012, Australia; phone: 61 2 9549 3000; email: hla@hlamgt.com.au

NATIONAL LIBRARY OF AUSTRALIA CIP DATA

Author:	Cornelius, Patricia.
Title:	Do not go gentle and The berry man: two plays / Patricia Cornelius.
ISBN:	9780868199078 (pbk.)
Other Authors/Contributors:	
	Cornelius, Patricia. Do not go gentle.
	Cornelius, Patricia. The berry man.
Dewey Number:	A822.3

Typeset by Dean Nottle for Currency Press.
Cover image and design by Emma Vine, Currency Press.
Front cover shows Rhys McConnochie as Scott in the 2010 fortyfivedownstairs production of *Do Not Go Gentle...* in Melbourne. (Photo: Jeff Busby)
Back cover shows Maude Davey as Marjorie and Greg Stone as Eric in the 2010 HotHouse Theatre production of *The Berry Man* at the Butter Factory Theatre, Wodonga. (Photo: Karen Donnelly)

Publication of this title was assisted by the Commonwealth Government through the Australia Council, its arts funding and advisory body.

Contents

DO NOT GO GENTLE…	1
Introduction *Julian Meyrick*	3
THE BERRY MAN	65
Introduction *Susie Dee*	67
Copying for Educational and Other Purposes	119

Currency Press acknowledges the Traditional Owners of the Country on which we live and work. We pay our respects to all Aboriginal and Torres Strait Islander Elders, past and present.

From rear: Malcolm Robertson as Oates, Pamela Rabe as Bowers, Anne Phelan as Wilson, Rhys McConnochie as Scott and Terry Norris as Evans in the 2010 fortyfivedownstairs production of DO NOT GO GENTLE… in Melbourne. (Photo: Jeff Busby)

ACKNOWLEDGMENTS

There are many people to thank who have given tremendous support to me as a playwright over the years. They are friends who have read and re-read, been read to, come to readings and have encouraged me, bolstered me, challenged me, annoyed me when they haven't said enough or when they've said too much.

Elvira Piantoni and Lesley Hall, in particular, I thank you for your belief in me. I thank my son, Lucci, who I have cornered and made sit and listen to pieces and who has offered me insightful comments before making his escape. I want to acknowledge the gang of six fellow theatre practitioners, whom I write and make work with and with whom I talk endlessly and passionately about theatre and how to make it powerful and how to make it mean something and how to deal with the culturally cringing and fearful industry we are part of. Andrew Bovell, Eugenia Fragos, Melissa Reeves, Christos Tsiolkas and Irine Vela, thank you.

And thank you to the two small theatre comanies who produced these plays. fortyfivedownstairs is an exceptional and courageous company who invest in new and Australian works and who took on *Do Not Go Gentle...* and fought to find the funding to support its wonderful production. Mary Lou Jelbart and Helen Rickards and the staff of fortyfive were extraordinary in their championing of the play and their powerful conviction is somewhat rare nowadays. HotHouse Theatre is a regional company and under the leadership of Charlie Parkins commissioned me to write *The Berry Man* and the company developed and supported the work to production. Small and medium range companies have mostly been defunded and I lament their loss. They have always been integral to the making of new Australian work.

Two directors, Julian Meyrick for *Do Not Go Gentle...*, and Susie Dee for *The Berry Man*, worked long and passionately to bring these plays to production. They are inspiring and inventive and make beautiful work. I thank them dearly.

Many thanks go to the many actors who participated in the workshop and readings of *Do Not Go Gentle...* and *The Berry Man*, and who helped make greater sense of the plays for me. And to Playwriting Australia who accepted *The Berry Man* for its workshop and festival program.

Finally, I thank Mark Wilkinson, who many years ago commissioned me to write a play called *Hogs Hairs and Leeches* which was the play that was the genesis for *Do Not Go Gentle*...

Patricia Cornelius

DO NOT GO GENTLE

Anne Phelan as Wilson and Rhys McConnochie as Scott in the 2010 fortyfivedownstairs production of DO NOT GO GENTLE... in Melbourne. (Photo: Jeff Busby)

Introduction

About the play

At the heart of all plays with something to say lies something that cannot be said. It is this ineffability, this silent soul, which gives drama its flavour, shape and force. It is what turns plays into memorable experiences. So it is with *Do Not Go Gentle...*, a play I was fortunate enough to work on for six years prior to its eventual production (despite all its awards and accolades, still just the one so far). During this time I saw Patricia, the writer, grapple with a series of dramatic problems both simple and profound. *Do Not Go Gentle...* is not a drama about aging. Or not only a drama about aging. It is a meditation on time, loss and love, on what it is to reach a point when a judgement on one's life is both unavoidable and beside the point. How to speak this truth? The truth of the ultimate worth of human life on the verge of certain demise?

Robert Falcon Scott's doomed expedition to the South Pole is as near a piece of public real estate as it is possible to get. Everyone knows the story—what the media call 'the myth'. Which means that, usefully for a playwright, it can be invoked without being explained. Its associations, of courage, comradeship, daring and determination, are entrained whenever the narrative is raised, even obliquely.

Now Australians don't take kindly to the heroic posture. We know too much about the real world to credit the larger-than-life claims of those who turn out, in the end, to be life-size after all. Scott has had his detractors. He was a fool, a monomaniac, an imperialist adventurer. But is it a question of being larger than life or being large enough to confront life's epic challenges? Of finding within ourselves the resources for a renewed humanity? We believe Scott had the courage to face his moment of no return. We hope he did. When the time comes, we hope we do too.

A metaphor works by taking two things that are unalike and juxtaposing them in such a way that a bond of meaning is forcibly established. Two things that in the real world do not belong together are brought together in imaginative manoeuvre to create new cognitive terrain. Like stars in a shared orbit the terms affect each other but remain apart. The distance between them creates a gravitational field that changes our understanding of their combination. In literary jargon, the metaphor thereby achieves 'uplift'. But exactly why this works is a deep and abiding mystery.

About the production

Six months before *Do Not Go Gentle...* went into rehearsals the actor Monica Maughan died. Monica had been a strong force in the development of the play, had done two of the Melbourne readings, and hoped to be cast in the final production. When it became clear she had a journey of her own to go on, she phoned up to vet my casting. She had a good eye, knew the field. I miss her and look for her on opening nights (she went to all she could). Her sudden death brought the play into vivid relief for me. The division of terms fundamental to metaphorical conceits is an unstable one, I discovered. Orbits crumble and stars crash into each other. It is the fate of metaphors to become real. That is what gives them their edge.

Trying to get *Do Not Go Gentle...* staged was a French farce with the laughs left out. After its initial reading on the Hard Lines development program at MTC in 2005, came three years of door knocking every major theatre in the country. Responses to the play ranged from the underwhelmed to the bewildered. The most positive was from Belvoir Company B, who twice considered it but felt there was 'something missing'. Now that *Do Not Go Gentle...* has won or been nominated for every major theatrical award it is clear the thing missing was the will to stage the play. But at least Belvoir read it, which was not true of the Australia Council, whose assessment procedures allowed only eleven pages of the script to be submitted. Why eleven, I wondered, as I fashioned my response to their rejection. We were playing with a stacked deck. No chance of *Do Not Go Gentle...* showing its worth under such conditions. I wrote:

> It is some time since I was directly concerned with Theatre Board priorities. Yet in one area I have been acutely conscious of its operations: that of new stage writing. My work as a literary

manager, dramaturge and director of Australian drama spans twenty years. In that period I have seen a deep, and to my mind erroneous division entrench itself between 'text-based' and 'non-text-based' theatrical performance. The persistence of these terms, at once fatuous and misleading, does not do justice to the type and variety of projects which lay claim, at core or in part, to a literary component. It is difficult to assess the qualities of a play off the page. It is far easier to assess a project's extra-dramatic features—its use of new technology, location, social context, creative personnel and/or target audience—than to engage in painstaking dramatic analysis. Yet, with some projects, this is exactly what is required to identify their originality, and *Do Not Go Gentle...* is a good example. For Patricia's play is not about old people in a naturalistic sense. It places an uncompromising metaphor on stage—that of a long, ultimately fatal trek to the South Pole—as a means of exposing, exploring and expanding our experience of the aging process. Again and again, talking to different companies about the play, I faced questions like 'why are the characters in the Antarctic?' and 'why doesn't Patricia show they are really in a nursing home?' But the characters aren't 'really' anywhere. They occupy a striking and independent poetic reality. In this, *Do Not Gentle...* is part of a sizeable and significant body of work—one that includes plays such as *Love* and *The Call*—which has seen Patricia loosen her ties to realist aesthetics without sacrificing dramatic coherence and force. This is where the cutting edge of Australian new stage writing lies, and the problems that define it should be widely understood. That they are not, signals a gap between the official idea of what constitutes 'the new' and the reality of innovatory dramatic practice as it is pursued by artists like Patricia in Australian theatre today.

(Letter to the Australia Council from J. Meyrick, 30 May 2009)

I must have hit a nerve. With our second grant application we got the money.

About the play

At first glance, the mark of Patricia's writing is its brazen theatricality, its rejection of realism and the resulting tonal, visual and physical freedom. Certainly, *Do Not Go Gentle...* is not interested in logically justifying its imaginative leaps. There are clues aplenty as to who the characters are in themselves (old men and women). But no attempt is made to exposit these, to render them consistent or suggest they are 'what is really going on'. What is 'really going on' in *Do Not Go Gentle...* outstrips any level of representation, fantastic or mundane—which is why only Scott's disastrous journey to the South Pole will do as a central conceit. One by one, the individual members of his expedition must leave it; must go off, alone, into the snow; onto whatever comes next.

But for me it is the truth Patricia fuses into her mind-boggling formal experimentation that promotes these characters to a superior level. The glory of the stage is that it can raise a metaphor to a level beyond everyday reality yet remain in touch with its underlying meaning. It can show us what is under our noses but eludes our attention. *Do Not Go Gentle...* is rich in acutely observed detail, in occasions for empathy that erupt like tiny, nuclear explosions: Wilson remembering how she was terrified of her father; Oates admitting he could not speak to his son; Evans outraged, even as an old man, at the injustice of the world; Bowers desperately trying to recall the names of objects in her office. There is a politics of sympathy at work here that militantly extends into the lives of the characters and demands they admit deep truths even as they ride a madcap journey of common delusion. It is the journey that releases them, though, that allows them to speak from the heart: as if imagination and reality were not opposed categories of experience, but somehow linked, somehow in cahoots (more mystery here).

The play never preaches. *Do Not Go Gentle...* has many things to say about sex, politics, regret, food, ballroom dancing and having fun. But the play is not in the business of summing up or thematising the ultimate object of its attention: the value of life in the face of the inevitability of death. There is not a sliver of sentimentality or false hope in the drama. Rather there is deep and deft intention in the mood of the piece, in something arising between and beyond its beautiful, poetic words. And in this intention there is a genuine response to life's sufferings and challenges and a silent prompt: to never be so afraid of death we forget to live.

About the production

Patricia's play would still be in the shoebox if it were not for fortyfivedownstairs and the courage and determination they showed in taking the play on when no-one else would look at it. When the average age of your cast is 73 years old you need support to tackle the problems that inevitably come your way. 'You can stand up now', I said to Rhys McConnochie and Annie Phelan one day, when they had finished rehearsing a love scene on their knees and were staying down longer than they ought. 'We're trying', they replied, struggling painfully upright. The accumulated years of stage experience under my remit, I worked out in an idle moment, was 385. It was terrific, but the play was hard work for everybody. MaryLou Jelbart, Helen Rickards and the staff of fortyfive were tireless, cheerful, generous and amazingly efficient in handling all aspects of the production. I've directed a few new Australian works in my time, but never one where play and management were in such accord. There was the usual trepidation as opening night loomed into view, the desire to please the playwright, to satisfy audiences, to escape the wrath of the critics. But no fear appended to the show itself, no sense of being held hostage by the need to achieve some extrinsic goal. fortyfive had no such goal. They wanted to stage the play. So they went ahead and did it.

The cast were amazing to work with, of course. An incomparable combination of strength and vulnerability. Great powers on the wane, all the greater for the fact of their passing. I was privileged to direct those actors and not an hour went by when I did not have evidence of it.

The achievement of all the cast was significant. But there are actors who helped in the development of the play who should also be acknowledged like Lewis Fiander and, of course, Monica. Sometimes I'd look around the rehearsal room half expecting to see her. Or I'd think I'd hear her voice. I'd forget she was dead. Her sharp but forgiving spirit would settle over me and guide my hand (I would imagine this,

this I would imagine) and I was possessed of the conviction that, despite the years of rebuff, and the difficulties that lay ahead, everything would be well.

This time we would return safe from our journey.

Julian Meyrick
September 2011

Julian Meyrick is a director and a theatre historian. He was Associate Director and Literary Adviser at Melbourne Theatre Company 2002–2007 and set up the Hard Lines play development program under which *Do Not Go Gentle…* was first presented..

Do Not Go Gentle… was first produced by fortyfivedownstairs, 45 Flinders Lane, Melbourne, on 6 August 2010, with the following cast:

ALEX / PETER	Paul English
MARIA	Jane Friedl
SCOTT	Rhys McConnochie
EVANS	Terry Norris
WILSON	Anne Phelan
BOWERS	Pamela Rabe
OATES	Malcolm Robertson

Director, Julian Meyrick
Designer, Marg Howell
Music and Sound Designer, Irine Vela
Lighting Designer, Richard Vabre

Patricia Cornelius is a Recipient of a Literature Board, Australia Council of the Arts grant and R.E. Ross Trust Award.

CHARACTERS

MARIA, in her 80s
SCOTT, in his 80s
WILSON (also known as MARY), in her 80s
BOWERS (also known as CLAUDIA, or BIRDIE), 52
EVANS (also known as TAFFY or THE STRONG MAN), in his 80s
OATES (also known as TITUS or SOLDIER), in his 80s
CREATURE (also known as PETER, son to OATES), 58
ALEX, husband to Claudia, 58 (doubled with PETER)
SCOT, Mary's husband (doubled with EVANS)

Actors over the age of 60 should be considered when casting the older parts.

SETTING

A fragile world.

Act One:
  On a field of ice
  In sleeping bags

Act Two:
  A labyrinth of crevasses and ice towers
  In sleeping bags

ACT ONE

SCENE ONE

An aurora provides a spectacular display of streamers of light, but the landscape, an expanse of ice, chills one to the bones—a cold, godforsaken place.

MARIA, *a diva, appears dressed in an elegant, full-length white gown. Her feet are bare on the ice.*

She sings: 'Va, Pensiero'—Giuseppi Verdi (from Nabucco*).*

Five figures appear. They walk slowly and rhythmically as they trudge across the ice. Their journey is hard, extremely hard, and the rhythm is mesmerising and seductive.

They wear polar gear of the early twentieth century: balaclavas, fur hats, their hands are buried in enormous fur mittens, their feet in reindeer boots, their leggings are strapped, and their bodies are shapeless with layers of clothing. Each of them wears a cloth harness.

The five trekkers come to a stop.

MARIA *finishes her song and disappears.*

The five stare out at the endless horizon. They are breathless. For some time they breathe as one, creating a peculiar song of their own.

SCOTT *finally speaks while his four companions remain fixated on the space before them.*

SCOTT: The final leg of our journey, and our courage and endurance is being tested in a way that has and will never be tested again. Five of us pitted against the power and treachery of the sea ice, the difficult surfaces of the snow, the biting winds and blizzards. Five of us terrorised by the hidden crevasses that appear like grins beneath our feet. Five of us, inexorably linked and yet utterly alone. There is no doubt that Amundsen's plan is a very serious menace to ours. He has a shorter distance to the Pole by sixty miles—I never thought he could have got so many dogs to the ice. His plan of running them seems excellent. Let's leg it, men.

No-one moves.

BOWERS: I'm cold.

EVANS: I'm cold.

OATES: I'm cold.

WILSON: I'm as warm as toast.

SCOTT: We have laid depots where we have buried horsemeat for our return. I felt some remorse when we dispatched Jehu, and Chinaman, even shooting the fiendish Christopher saddened me a little, but their meat will cook up to a welcomed hoosh for our return journey.

BOWERS: The meat's as tough as an old boot.

EVANS: It's cheap.

OATES: I can't bite through it, not with my teeth.

WILSON: It is a little chewy but it's not too bad.

SCOTT: After a month of wordless plodding to the crunch of hoof and boot we are rewarded by a breathtaking panorama. Mount Markham towers above us, rising fourteen thousand feet into a clear blue sky. Everyone is in excellent spirits.

EVANS: What the hell are we doing here?

BOWERS: I don't belong here.

OATES: In this godforsaken place.

WILSON: I don't mind it myself.

SCOTT: Across undulating ice ridges up to twenty-five feet high we inch our way up the thirty-mile-wide, nine-thousand-foot-high Beardmore Glacier, towing twelve weeks' of food and oil. There's no escaping the crevasses, but to tell the truth, I find it decidedly exciting not knowing which step will give way.

OATES: I can't sleep at night.

WILSON: It's the groaning.

OATES: And the wheezes.

EVANS: And the farts. Trumpeting arseholes!

BOWERS: I shouldn't be here.

WILSON: I enjoy the company.

SCOTT: After months of deliberation, I've chosen my team. No horses, no dogs, no motorised sledges, only men: myself and four of the finest.

BOWERS: Where exactly are we?

SCOTT: Bowers. Always hungry for adventure, a fat little man with short legs and a perfectly immense nose, thus christened 'Birdie'.

BOWERS: I don't know this place.
SCOTT: He fell down the main hatch on the ship onto a bed of pig iron and walked away and the legend of the indestructible Bowers was born.
BOWERS: I don't know where I am.
SCOTT: The best navigator by far who also keeps the expedition's meteorological records.
EVANS: Nobody tells me where to go.
SCOTT: Edgar Evans. 'Taffy', he's called. Also known as 'The Strong Man'.
EVANS: Nobody tells me what to do.
SCOTT: A good-natured fellow, full of high spirits and great humour.
EVANS: I'd bloody well knock his block off if he did.
SCOTT: I do not think that harder men or better sledge travellers ever took the trail as Bowers and Evans.
OATES: This place gives me the horrors.
SCOTT: Oates. We call him 'Titus'. The only army man in the expedition. Sometimes I call him 'Soldier'. [*To* OATES] Hey, Soldier.
OATES: [*under his breath*] Don't call me that.
SCOTT: No better man with horses. Not so good with words but there's little out here to be said. Words tend to stay tucked up warm inside.
WILSON: I think it's quite a nice day.
SCOTT: And Wilson. A great friend, a soul mate, he ranks very high in the scale of human beings. He's also a fine doctor.
WILSON: Could be a little sunnier, of course.
SCOTT: Wilson's inclusion was made because of his medical acumen. And like the others, because of his pulling power.
EVANS: It's bloody cold.
OATES: I'm chilled to the core.
BOWERS: It's in my bones.
EVANS: My hands, I can't feel them.
OATES: It's as cold as...
ALL: Ice.
SCOTT: Ice and more ice. The beauty of it astounds me. Look, men, look, a glistening world without edges, a world that invites us to cross it, to discover it, and to widen our ever-diminishing horizons. Can you see it?

They look.

You must.

WILSON: I can see it. It's absolutely lovely.

BOWERS: I see it.

OATES: And I.

EVANS: I too see it.

SCOTT: It's what keeps us alive.

Together they take a large breath.

To the Pole where we'll plant our flag and fire the imaginations of generations to come.

They trudge on.

SCENE TWO

An ungodly howl echoes across the landscape.

OATES *runs across the ice. He is terrified and runs as if pursued. He stops to catch his breath.*

OATES: Come out, God damn you! Show yourself. [*He turns in a circle expecting his pursuer to appear.*] Do I look wealthy? My pockets are empty, believe me, anything I have had of worth has been taken from me. [*He stops and listens.*] I know you're there. I've seen your tracks. I've spotted you way off in the distance: a wild, strange thing, not man, not creature, something straight from hell. And I hear you.

He listens. There's a faint sound, something like a howl. OATES *grows agitated.*

Show yourself or leave me be. Is it the meat on my bones you want? Come, feast on me.

Again the terrible howl. OATES *weeps.*

There's nothing I can do for you. I can't help you.

A figure appears in silhouette and moves slowly toward him.

At last! For God's sake, who or what are you?

SCOTT *throws back his fur hood.*

SCOTT: What are you doing, Titus? Come into the tent, man, or you'll freeze where you stand.

OATES: Can't you hear it? You must hear that bloody sound…
SCOTT: Do you mean the crack of the ice, or the snap in the air, or the chugging of one's breath?
OATES: I mean the howling.
SCOTT: There's no howling, Soldier. What out there could howl apart from the wind and today there's not a wisp to push us along.
OATES: Maybe a dog.
SCOTT: A dog out there alone on the ice in weather like this, I don't think so.
OATES: Some other creature, then.
SCOTT: Nothing out there lives.
OATES: A boy.
SCOTT: A boy! Come inside, Soldier, it's not the wind but your brain playing tricks.
OATES: I've heard of it before. A baby stolen, or abandoned by its mother, taken by wolves or jackals or some other creature and brought up as one of their own. Running on all fours, it's swift and it hunts and speaks a wild creature's language.
SCOTT: No such boy lives here, Soldier.
OATES: Don't call me that! I'm not a soldier, you got that? I don't want you to call me that.
SCOTT: Come inside, Oates. You need company and good cheer.

> SCOTT *exits.* OATES *looks about him. He calls defiantly to the creature across the plateau.*

OATES: There are no trees! Do you hear me?! Not a tree in sight!

> *He follows* SCOTT *off.*

> *A strange silhouette appears, half man, half animal. He howls mournfully and lopes away.*

SCENE THREE

SCOTT, WILSON, EVANS, BOWERS *and* OATES, *in sledge-pulling formation. They wear harnesses pulled tight on their chests as they lean forward against them. The reins are attached way back in the distance. They pull as one, an almighty pull. And again. And again.*

SCOTT: Pull! Pull! Pull! Starting requires ten to fifteen desperate jerks on the harness to move the sledge at all. Pull!

They pull once more and are met with success. They cheer. They lift their feet and trudge hard.

The best people for any expedition are the most naturally competitive individuals. How many miles today, gentlemen?

EVANS: Let's see how many before you fall flat on your face.

SCOTT: You'll find me still standing at the end of this race, Evans.

BOWERS: You've all got longer legs and still you can't keep up.

SCOTT: But can you last, Bowers? Can you last?

OATES: We'll march till we drop. Put as much distance as possible between me and the devil who stalks me.

SCOTT: I'm surprised how easy it is to keep up with you younger, stronger men.

WILSON: I enjoy a good brisk walk.

SCOTT: Call that brisk, Wilson? I call it dawdling.

OATES: [*looking over his shoulder*] Let's leave the heinous thing for dead.

SCOTT: Put your shoulders into it. You're as slow as wet rags.

EVANS: Jesus Christ! What do you want? Blood?

SCOTT: The act of competing, man against man, hour after hour, day after day, can cause hostility between team members.

EVANS: Do you want to wear us out?

SCOTT: A small price to pay for success.

EVANS: Who in hell do you think you are?

WILSON: I love the fresh air and the wind in my hair.

SCOTT: The faster and longer the team travels each day, the shorter the period taken to reach our goal. Come on, lads, step out. Put some muscle in your stride.

They march, long and hard they pull against their reins and a sense of competitiveness sets in. EVANS *is incensed at the pace* SCOTT *sets.*

EVANS: What are we? Oxen, to be driven, to be beaten, to be bullied? No, animals are treated with greater respect. Are we slaves owned by a pharaoh who has cut out our tongues? No, our tongues are in our heads lying idle. There's no whip, nor is there a sword in the small of our backs. Are we zombies? Did someone remove our brains whilst we slept? Are we mad, then? Do we trip and grin, and nod and beg for further hardships against us? No. Fools, that's what we are, who can't stand up to a man who is clearly cracked.

SCOTT *pushes ahead.*

SCOTT: You're dragging behind!
EVANS: The immense shove of the man. He leads us on remorselessly.
SCOTT: Keep up!
EVANS: It's a walk, do you hear me?
SCOTT: Pull! Pull!
EVANS: We're not mules, for God's sake. We're bags of rattling bones.
SCOTT: What distance, Bowers?
BOWERS: What?
SCOTT: The distance.
BOWERS: [*making it up*] Fourteen and three-quarter miles, how about that?
SCOTT: Let's round it off. Make it fifteen.
BOWERS: Fifteen, sixteen, twenty, forty, I don't care.
SCOTT: That's the spirit, Bowers.
OATES: The further the better.
WILSON: I enjoy our walks.
EVANS: Fools, we are.
WILSON: It helps pass the time.
EVANS: When to shower, when to eat, when to sleep, when to turn out the light. Next we'll be told when to shit!
OATES: Keep it clean.
SCOTT: Pull! Pull!
EVANS: I'm not putting up with this crap.
SCOTT: There are still no sign of Norwegian tracks.

SCENE FOUR

A blizzard. It is silent. MARIA *is alone. She wears a forties-style, off-white, woollen skirt and jacket. She carries a suitcase. Her feet are bare. She is clearly disorientated, lost in the storm.*

MARIA: I can't see. I can't see. Excuse me. Could you help me please? I can't see. It's the dust. It won't stop falling. Without a sound it falls. Eerily. The dust has blinded me. I can't find the kitchen table. My entire family fits under it while we wait until the dust clears. [*She crosses the space clumsily.*] I am told to pack. I grab at this and I grab at that. I think, should I take this sweater, this pair of shoes, will I need more socks, tops, an overcoat, although it's summer? What about my red hat? Will I take this photograph or will the glass crack? And I look for something more and I don't know what it is, but I must take it, I must find it. It must be packed. Finally I close my case and I run through the house and I see my mother has left her scarf on the back of a chair, a postcard from my aunt lies on the dresser there, a packet of pins, a ball, a button torn from my sister's blouse which I try to pick up but my fingernails are bitten short and it slides onto the floor. I force myself to go out the door and down the path and out onto the street. But the trucks have gone. And they have taken my family. [*She looks about and is daunted by the space around her.*] Excuse me, but I don't know this place. I don't belong here. I have no idea how I came to be here. There's been a dreadful mistake. This is not my country, this enormous empty space I hate.

SCENE FIVE

The five trekkers are cocooned inside their sleeping bags with only their faces visible. Like chrysalises, they hang. The storm rages outside. It dies down at times, only to suddenly surge again. The cocoons are buffeted slightly.

WILSON: If you don't want to play anymore, we won't.
EVANS: 'I spy', 'I spy'. For God's sake, what's there to see?
WILSON: Alright, we'll talk, then.
BOWERS: I don't want to be asked a whole lot of questions.
OATES: I've nothing to say.
SCOTT: I've heard you talk endlessly on the subject of horses, Titus.
EVANS: I've plenty to say, about the conditions here for starters. They're deplorable. Are we going to stand by and…?
WILSON: While we're stuck here, let's take the chance to get to know a little about each other.
OATES: I like apples.
EVANS: There's never anything fresh to eat. No fruit, no green vegetables, no…
BOWERS: Cheese, I love cheese.
OATES: I miss garlic of all things.
BOWERS: It's cheese I love.

SCOTT: What I'd do for something sweet.
BOWERS: I like a lolly every now and then.
EVANS: I'd give my right arm for some chocolate.
OATES: I ate a dozen pink meringues once. Crushed them in my mouth one by one.
WILSON: I had in mind talk of a more intimate nature.
SCOTT: Right, Wilson, right. How are everyone's toes?
OATES: My feet hurt.
EVANS: I can't feel my hands.
SCOTT: I've some chafing under my arms where the harness rubs.
BOWERS: My digestion—
WILSON: Not about our health. We could talk about ourselves, about what we wanted from life, perhaps.
EVANS: You want to talk about self-indulgent, bourgeois crap. The world is suffering, all about you is misery, for fuck's sake, and—
SCOTT: Evans!
OATES: Keep it clean.
SCOTT: Wilson is attempting to make the time wasted, while this storm rages on interminably, slightly more bearable. Go ahead, Wilson, lead the way.
WILSON: I think I expected it to be something else. I think I expected it to be more. I think I'm rather disappointed, actually.
EVANS: Of course you are. You've been cheated.
BOWERS: [*suddenly irritated*] What did you do, hang around and wait for something good to happen? You can't wait. You've got to make things happen.
EVANS: Not everyone is in a position to make things happen.
OATES: There's no controlling what happens. Things just happen. Whether you like it or not, they just happen.
WILSON: That's true, walking along a street, a bough from a perfectly healthy tree decides to fall on your head.
SCOTT: You trudge along what you think is good solid ice and all of a sudden you plummet hundreds of metres down a crevasse below.
EVANS: We're not talking about natural bloody disasters.
BOWERS: You have to make the most of life.
EVANS: I agree with you.
BOWERS: Take it by the scruff of the neck.

EVANS: And shake it.
BOWERS: It's entirely up to you whether you make a success of it or not.
EVANS: I couldn't disagree with you more.
BOWERS: No-one's going to do it for you, if you want something from life you go out and get it.
EVANS: You talk as if we're all the same. We're not.
BOWERS: There's nothing stopping anyone from making their life a success.
EVANS: Of course there is. There are plenty of reasons: opportunity for one. Not all of us are born into the privileged classes.
BOWERS: I'm sick to death of hearing people whining about their disadvantages. I had bloody cardboard in my shoes too. So what?
EVANS: Oh, I see, you think because you pulled yourself out of the trough then anyone who is left in it must be a lazy slob.
BOWERS: That's exactly what I think, actually.
EVANS: You think because you made it then there's no reason why we can't all make it.
BOWERS: Yes, I do. I think, get off your bloody fat bottoms and make a go of it.
EVANS: Good on you, join forces with the upper classes and happily absorb their ideas of the worthy and the worthless.
BOWERS: Why shouldn't I? I worked for it. I deserve it.
EVANS: You'll never belong. They'll use you up and they'll throw you out. On the rubbish heap, the moment you stuff up.
WILSON: Oh, dear me, forget it, let's just talk about the weather.
BOWERS: What's your problem?
EVANS: Nothing like a meaty discussion.
BOWERS: And it's just heating up.
WILSON: Oh, I see. Don't mind me.
BOWERS: I got myself my first job and I worked like a bloody dog. I made it impossible to be ignored. I was efficient, plucky, on the ball. Things happened for me because I made them happen.
EVANS: You think life's about having to work like a dog?
WILSON: [*to* BOWERS] What were you?

Slight pause.

BOWERS: Never mind what I was. What I was, was accomplished.

WILSON: I would've liked to be something like that.
BOWERS: And there were plenty who thought a woman shouldn't be rewarded for the work she did.
WILSON: Well, we are different really, aren't we?
BOWERS: Why? What stopped you from making something of your life?
WILSON: Me? [*Pause.*] I didn't realise I could.
EVANS: When you're poor, how are you meant to know that life could be more?
WILSON: I've never been poor.
BOWERS: What stopped you from doing whatever you wanted to do?
WILSON: I didn't know what I wanted. I didn't know that I could want.
BOWERS: Everybody wants. Rich or poor, we all want.
WILSON: I don't remember ever wanting.
BOWERS: Honestly! How can that be? Never wanting.
EVANS: She obviously had everything.
WILSON: Perhaps I did. I remember my childhood with sweetness. I never wanted for anything.
BOWERS: You said that life disappointed you.
WILSON: I must have wanted more.
OATES: Not everyone can make something of their life.
EVANS: Everyone should be given the chance.
OATES: Life can't always be satisfying.
EVANS: Why not?
WILSON: You'd think it could be stimulating, at least.
OATES: You can't control terrible things from happening.
EVANS: You can try.
OATES: You can't control wars. They're beyond control. Nothing you can do about wars.
WILSON: No, that's true, terrible things, wars.
EVANS: You can stop fuelling them with young working-class men who don't know their arse from their elbows…
OATES: You have to do your bit.
EVANS: … who haven't got a clue why they're in uniform…
OATES: Have to honour your country and that.
EVANS: … or where they're going or why…
OATES: Do something bigger than yourself.
EVANS: … or who they're pointing a gun at.

OATES: Can't all be about take. Got to give something back, to make a contribution.
EVANS: How is killing or being killed contributing anything?
WILSON: I would've liked to have offered my services to the war effort.
BOWERS: Oh, you would have been a great help.
OATES: To put yourself on the line, to put your life at risk because your country is worth dying for.
WILSON: It would be wonderful to be asked to do something like that.
EVANS: You're dying alright, but in battles that have nothing to do with you.
OATES: Just once in your life.
EVANS: War's a terrible, terrible thing.
OATES: It does ask a lot of you.
EVANS: For death, that's all it asks
OATES: Yes, it asks for that. It definitely asks for that.

The storm suddenly lulls.

SCOTT: Listen to yourselves. Here we are, on an expedition that has taken us into unknown lands, towards the discovery of the South Pole, where we will hoist our country's flag and be the first to do so in the entire world. What we're doing is most extraordinary, most profound, and we'll be remembered for all eternity. And why are we here? Not because of monetary gain, nor for a ridiculous grab for fame. We're here for no other reason than because it is something grand, it's for one's country, for its honour, for the world to see we can. You're experiencing all you could yearn for in life and, unbelievably, you don't appear to be aware of it.

Silence. The four trekkers appear to have fallen asleep.

Now, I suggest we get some sleep. I pray tomorrow will bring us a clear day. It won't be long, lads, before the Pole is ours.

SCOTT *sleeps.* WILSON *opens her eyes and hisses at* BOWERS.

BOWERS: What? What do you think you're doing?
WILSON: What happened?
BOWERS: What?
WILSON: Why are you here?
BOWERS: Why shouldn't I be here?
WILSON: Why?

BOWERS: I said I didn't want to be asked a whole lot of silly questions.
WILSON: You're not old enough.
BOWERS: If you keep disturbing me I will ask to be moved to a different room.

> BOWERS *turns away and closes her eyes.*

WILSON: Why are you here?

SCENE SIX

The blizzard has cleared. WILSON *emerges from a tent that is almost entirely buried in snow. She wanders out onto the ice plateau. She lifts her arms and breathes in the air. She feels suddenly hot and begins to take off layers of clothing and finally stands in her pants and bra, and balaclava and fur boots. She closes her eyes, lifts her head as if to the sun, and smiles a beatific smile.*

WILSON: Ah, that feels so much better.

> SCOTT *emerges from the tent. He's aware of* WILSON*'s presence but is so deeply absorbed in his own thoughts he doesn't actually see her.*

SCOTT: Three days and nights of raging chaos. What on earth does such weather mean, this time of year?
WILSON: It's glorious.
SCOTT: The blizzard has set us back. All the wishing in the world will not push Amundsen and his dogs off the Antarctic continent.

> WILSON *turns slowly in a circle.*

WILSON: The sun on my skin. I'm like some cat turning in circles to soak it in.
SCOTT: Sky and snow merges into a single pall of whiteness.
WILSON: I can't tell you how long it's been. Years and years. Perhaps not since I was a kid.
SCOTT: I have to hand it to you, Wilson, first up, out and about, tending to your collections diligently.
WILSON: I stripped off and danced under the sprinkler on the front lawn. I was twelve years old. Oh, my God, not a stitch on, and there I was, giggling hysterically, lifting my knees. My small breasts…

SCOTT: A finer pair of penguin eggs I've never seen. Emperors, aren't they? Splendid specimens for your collection.
WILSON: Probably the only time in my entire life I have ever felt free.
SCOTT: Your rocks, Wilson, how's your collection progressing?
WILSON: For a few moments, very few. Laughing for no particular reason, feeling close to glee, I think you'd call it.
SCOTT: Your contribution to understanding a completely uninvestigated land will one day be honoured, I promise you.
WILSON: And then my body became a stranger to me.
SCOTT: Antarctica is a land of mystery, less is known about it than we know about the moon.
WILSON: I don't know it. It's a secret kept from me.
SCOTT: You remind me why we're really here. It's the work that counts, not the applause. Your rocks, Wilson, it would give me great pleasure to see them.

He turns and is astounded at the vision of WILSON *in her underwear.*

Wilson! Are you trying to kill yourself? What the hell do you think you're doing?
WILSON: I'm basking, Scot.
SCOTT: You're what?
WILSON: Basking. Basking.
SCOTT: But the cold… I don't understand.
WILSON: I'm hot.
SCOTT: Hot!
WILSON: I am. Feel me, I'm hot.
SCOTT: I've seen fingers split, toes blacken, lips blister and noses bitten. Within seconds I've seen sores pour pus, fingernails lift, tongues split, and fingers charred black. I've seen a man with his eyelids frozen open, unable to blink. If I was not here standing looking at you I would never believe it. You're almost naked, Wilson, and there isn't anything wrong with you. You're not even bloody shivering. Not a blister to be seen. You look perfect.
WILSON: Really?
SCOTT: You look superb.
WILSON: Thank you.
SCOTT: Truly magnificent.
WILSON: Me, Scot, magnificent?

SCOTT: Absolutely.
WILSON: Why don't you join me?
SCOTT: What?
WILSON: Take off your clothes, Scot.
SCOTT: Not a chance, Wilson.
WILSON: I know you must be shocked. But truly, why not?
SCOTT: I'd die, Wilson, I'd die in a matter of minutes.
WILSON: What's the harm? It's perfectly natural, after all. It's just us. No-one else will see us.
SCOTT: I couldn't face it, Wilson, I know it.
WILSON: Oh, Scot, please join me. Don't make me feel foolish.
SCOTT: Foolish! You're a wonder, a marvel. There is no scientific explanation for your resistance, you're endurance is incredible.
WILSON: It is rather, isn't it? I think I have endured a great deal. I think the trick is not to think of it as such. To get on with it.
SCOTT: Your skin, Wilson, it has a lovely sheen, as if it's warm. I can't believe you're not freezing. My impulse is to wrap my arms about you.
WILSON: Go with it.
SCOTT: What?
WILSON: Go with this impulse of yours.
SCOTT: You mean…
WILSON: Please.

    SCOTT *wraps himself around her.*

SCOTT: This is ridiculous, you are warming me.

SCENE SEVEN

SCOTT *and his companions fan out, their harnesses pulled tight. It is as if they are frozen in trekking motion as they contemplate their thoughts.* EVANS *lunges forward, leaning hard against his harness.*

EVANS: Rage. Rage. Rage.
SCOTT: The lofty desolation of the polar plateau forces us in on our own thoughts.
EVANS: Rage against that which divides us, that which pits worker against worker, against shameless and brutal exploitation.

SCOTT: Each man wrapped and trapped within himself.

EVANS: Rage against injustice. It warms me in a cold, miserably cold world where some wear mink and others no coat at all.

SCOTT: Each minute and hour seems an eternity.

OATES *pulls at his harness.*

OATES: He's been following me for days. He thinks he's clever but I see him, a black dot in the distance. He's persistent.

SCOTT: Ever-repeated anxieties gnaw at the mind and vie with the dull throb of frostbitten fingers.

BOWERS *pulls at her harness.*

BOWERS: Leave at seven, left at the gate, wait at stop eighty-eight.

OATES: Sometimes I can almost see his form, a loping man-beast.

WILSON *pulls at her harness.*

WILSON: There is something I wanted.

BOWERS: Take the three-twelve tram, count fifteen stops, walk downhill two blocks.

OATES: He's a creature straight from hell.

WILSON: I remembered it just now.

BOWERS: Enormous brass numbers, seventy-two, through the automatic doors and up the lift to the fifty-fourth floor. Down the corridor. [*She waves.*] Hello, hello, hello.

WILSON: It came to me from a place I must have put under lock and key. It's funny how I forgot it. I wanted to kill my father. Of all the things a young woman could want and that was it.

SCOTT: Despite the bamboozling effects of the altitude, we are averaging thirteen miles a day by man-haul.

WILSON: I wouldn't have minded slipping some Drano into his drink, for instance, or giving him a good thwack to his head, with a brick, say, or something as heavy as that.

BOWERS: By the window is my desk, my computer, my calendar. Immediately change the date. Check my diary: interviews with thieves and murderers, with clergymen and torturers, and with politicians, the most boring of men.

EVANS: Rage. It's kept me heated, alright. I've told bosses where to shove it, stood up at meetings and screamed till I was blue in the face

because they were lying, because they were cheating, because they were taking us for chumps.
BOWERS: Adjust the photograph of... someone.
WILSON: I think there's some terrible complaint you can get that makes you want to kill your father, some Greek thing.
BOWERS: Forget the photograph, it doesn't matter.
OATES: [*calling*] Leave me be, can't you?! Leave me be!
EVANS: I've been called righteous and bombastic, a zealot, idealist, dirty commie bastard, mad Trotskyite. Yes, I say, that's me and me and me. So what? You think you've got a cowering shadow of a man here? Not likely. Fire in the belly, that's what I've got. It's a veritable furnace in here.
SCOTT: In the right direction, Bowers, I hope?
BOWERS: [*defensively*] Yes, of course. I know exactly where we're going.
WILSON: I wouldn't have minded stabbing him, quickly, there and there. Or push him off a cliff, I could do that easily.
SCOTT: The sun's ultraviolet rays, reflected off the snow, burn not only our corneas but also any exposed skin. Especially our lips which crack and bleed.
WILSON: It's not the kind of thing I'd tell people readily. I can see how awful it makes me look. Because he never lifted a hand to hurt me, he never interfered with me or any of that stuff. It seems quite unreasonable to want to kill him, but I did, I feared him that much.
SCOTT: Our faces are pocked with blisters and scabs.
EVANS: Rage, I feel it, it's running hot. I'll feel it till the day injustice stops.
SCOTT: The elements have aged us so.

They march on in a slow and mesmerising rhythm.

SCENE EIGHT

A terrified OATES *is pursued by a half man, half animal, across the ice. The* CREATURE *pulls* OATES *to the ground and they roll in a flailing, snarling ball.* OATES *manages to extricate himself and back away while the* CREATURE *prepares for a renewed attack.*

OATES: So, creature, the time has finally come. You have your prey; you have hunted patiently and persistently and won.

The CREATURE *growls menacingly.*

I'm yours. I give myself up. I can no longer run.

Again the CREATURE *growls.*

What kind of creature are you? Part beast, part man. Are you some primitive yet to be discovered? Hidden away some place that no-one's uncovered. I thought every inch of the Earth had been scratched away at, that there were no surprises like you to be had.

He leans forward and looks closely into the CREATURE*'s eyes. The* CREATURE *bares its teeth.*

No, that's not you. You're something else entirely. You're something that belongs to me, I see. I know you.

He tentatively extends his hand toward the animal.

Here we go, here we go. Yes? Yes? Here we are.

The CREATURE *snarls and bites at* OATES*' hand.*

Jesus! Take me, then. Get it over and done with and tear me limb from limb.

They stare at one another, waiting for the next move. Again OATES *extends his hand.*

No, not yet, hey? No? Want to make me shake a little longer. Keep my heart racing. Is that it? Take your time, there's no rush, I guess. Hey? Hey?

He almost touches the CREATURE *but again he bites at him and* OATES *quickly withdraws his hand.*

Ho ho ho ho ho, you're no easy take. No pushover, you. It would take a lot more to win you over. Can you be tamed, I wonder? Can you? Can you understand a word? By God, you look as if you do.

Again OATES *extends his hand.*

[*With great tenderness*] Do you think you can forgive me? Could you possibly find it in your heart to forgive me?

The CREATURE *snarls and slowly moves his nose towards* OATES*' hand. He licks it.*

SCENE NINE

An old and tinny pianola pumps out a waltz which surges and sags with an irregular tread.

The lights are strange on the ice, dappling and moving like they could be lighting an old dance floor.

MARIA *and* WILSON *step out onto the ice from different directions at the same time. They stop and look at one another.*

WILSON: Hello. I don't think we've met. Do you come here often?

MARIA: I don't want to be here.

WILSON: It will be only a matter of time before you'll feel perfectly at home.

MARIA: I will never feel at home here.

WILSON: The way I deal with it is to think of myself as some sort of gypsy. Wherever I am, I'm at home.

MARIA: Gypsies live in caravans.

WILSON: We used to have one of those. Every year my husband would drop me, the children and the caravan at Rosebud and join us on weekends when he could.

MARIA: I want to go home.

WILSON: I missed my house too, at first. I brought up my children there. I had collected every rock myself to build up my garden. My iris collection was the envy of the neighbourhood. I knew every nook and cranny of that house. I thought I'd die there. But to tell the truth it took me very little time before I forgot it. It's much easier that way.

MARIA: I will never forget.

WILSON: I lived there my entire adult life, and I did. [*She hears the music.*] Oh, listen to that, it's too lovely to resist.

    She offers MARIA *her hands.*

Shall we?

    With WILSON *leading, they begin to waltz.*

What better way to stop feeling homesick? Close your eyes and you could be dancing in your lounge room.

MARIA: With Stellios.

WILSON: I am dancing with Scot, but he's standing on my toes. I've changed partners, and my daughter, Anne, is dancing with me. She's quite good too, for a girl her age.
MARIA: My Stellios, he could dance. I always thought he was a bit of a ratbag. But after I danced with him…
WILSON: You thought he was divine.
MARIA: I did. He'd hold me close, like this.

    MARIA *pulls* WILSON *in close as they dance.*

WILSON: Oh, my.
MARIA: He'd lean his body into mine and I felt…
WILSON: Oh, my.
MARIA: The only people you have danced with are a man who stomped on your feet and a child. This is tragic.
WILSON: I have often danced with the man of my dreams.

    Dancing closely.

MARIA: And did he dance like this?
WILSON: Yes.

    MARIA *swings* WILSON *in a lovely move.*

MARIA: And like this?
WILSON: Yes.

    She swings WILSON *again.*

MARIA: And this?
WILSON: Oh, yes.
MARIA: I met my Stellios at Stretton's in High Street. I went with my friend, Natasha. We liked to dance. We worked in a hosiery factory and it was a way to unwind and to show off the stockings we got cheap. And, of course, when you dance you don't have to speak.

    MARIA *and* WILSON *have fitted together well now and dance beautifully for a few moments.*

I married him. He spoke Greek and I spoke Serbian. I learned a bit of his and him a bit of mine, but mostly we spoke English. For the kids. Stellios always believed this country would be our home.
WILSON: How absolutely wonderful.
MARIA: Wonderful? No.
WILSON: It's so romantic.

MARIA: Only on the dance floor.
WILSON: Your life is so interesting. Mine is rather dull.
MARIA: It is very dull not to be able to speak to anyone, your husband, your children, really speak to them.

She suddenly stops dancing.

I want to go home.
WILSON: Perhaps Stellios will visit soon.
MARIA: He's dead. Years ago.
WILSON: I'm sorry. Perhaps your children…
MARIA: I do not belong. I do not.
WILSON: This is your home now. I'm afraid you will have to accept your lot.

MARIA *grows more and more emotional.* WILSON *becomes agitated.*

MARIA: [*loudly*] I want to go home.
WILSON: Keep your voice down or you'll upset everyone.
MARIA: I want to go home.
WILSON: There's nothing wrong with it here.
MARIA: I want to go home.
WILSON: You're being silly.
MARIA: I want to go home.
WILSON: [*snapping*] What right have you to carry on?
MARIA: [*loudly and rebelliously*] I want to go home!
WILSON: Oh, for goodness sake, go, go on, go bloody home, you don't belong.

SCENE TEN

BOWERS *enters. She follows the map inside her head.*

BOWERS: Leave at seven, left at the gate, wait at stop eighty-eight. Take the three-twelve tram. Count fifteen stops. Walk down the hill two blocks. Enormous brass numbers, seventy-two, through the door and up the lift to the fifty-fourth floor. Down the corridor. [*She waves.*] Hello, hello, hello. By the window is my desk, my computer, my calendar… Change the date. Check my diary: interviews with thieves and murderers, with clergymen, with torturers, and with politicians, the most boring of men. Adjust the photograph of… someone. Forget the photograph, it doesn't matter.

From a distance a man's voice repeatedly calls, 'Claudia'. ALEX, *a man in his 50s, enters. He stands behind* BOWERS *and stares at her. She does not see him.*

ALEX: Claudia.
BOWERS: I know exactly where I am.
ALEX: Claudia. It's me.

BOWERS *turns and when she sees the man she takes fright.*

It's alright, it's only me.
BOWERS: Who are you?
ALEX: You know me.
BOWERS: I don't.
ALEX: You know me.
BOWERS: I don't.
ALEX: Surely you do.
BOWERS: I don't know you.
ALEX: Not even a little?
BOWERS: I've never met you in my life.
ALEX: Claudia, who am I?
BOWERS: Don't you know who you are?
ALEX: Yes, I know who I am. I'm Alex.
BOWERS: I don't know anyone named Alex.
ALEX: It doesn't sound familiar to you?
BOWERS: Not at all.
ALEX: Are you sure?
BOWERS: Yes, I'm sure. Of course I'm sure. Why wouldn't I be sure?
ALEX: We've known each other a long time.
BOWERS: I don't know you.
ALEX: Look at me.
BOWERS: You're frightening me.
ALEX: I don't mean to. Look at me.
BOWERS: You're frightening me.
ALEX: What about Anna? Do you know her? Or Jonathan?
BOWERS: I don't know who they are.
ALEX: They're children.
BOWERS: Children?
ALEX: Yes.
BOWERS: I don't know them.

ALEX: Anna and Jonathan are your...

    BOWERS *silences him uttering a terrible cry.*

BOWERS: You're frightening me.
ALEX: Yes, I know.
BOWERS: You know?
ALEX: I can see.
BOWERS: Well, don't.
ALEX: I'll stop.
BOWERS: Yes, stop.
ALEX: I have.
BOWERS: You've mistaken me for someone else.

    Pause.

ALEX: Yes, perhaps I have.
BOWERS: I'm sorry.
ALEX: I'm sorry too.
BOWERS: I hope you find her soon.
ALEX: I hope so too.
BOWERS: Yes, well, good luck to you.
ALEX: But I think she's gone for good.
BOWERS: Oh well, never mind.
ALEX: She was everything to me.
BOWERS: I'm sorry for your loss.
ALEX: [*whispering*] Claudia. Claudia.
BOWERS: For God's sake, you said she's gone.
ALEX: I thought perhaps she might come back.
BOWERS: If she's gone, she's gone.
ALEX: You're absolutely right.
BOWERS: She's gone. She's bloody gone.
ALEX: Right. Thank you.
BOWERS: Don't thank me; it's logical, that's all.
ALEX: I won't bother you again.
BOWERS: Good, I've enough to worry about.
ALEX: I won't come again.
BOWERS: Well, there's no point, is there?
ALEX: No, I guess not.
BOWERS: Goodbye, then.

ALEX: Goodbye.

> ALEX *continues to look at* BOWERS, *which unsettles her.*

BOWERS: Goodbye, goodbye.
ALEX: Goodbye.

> CLAUDIA *turns her back on him and* ALEX *exits.*

SCENE ELEVEN

SCOTT: We march on.

> *Shoulder to shoulder, the expedition of five marches on.*

January sixth, at ten thousand five hundred feet we come upon unusually bad sastrugi fields—a sea of fishhook waves making travel extremely difficult. I am dismayed to learn that Taff Evans has a nasty cut on his hand. My God, what have you done, Evans?

EVANS: What have I done? I've done my utmost, that's what I've done.

> *They march on.*

SCOTT: January ninth, we reach eighty-eight degrees, only ninety-five miles from the Pole.

> OATES *is looking back in the direction they have come, whistling to call in the creature.*

OATES: [*plaintively*] Where are you, boy?
SCOTT: Oates seems to be feeling the cold and fatigue.
OATES: Come on, fella. Keep up.
SCOTT: How goes it, Soldier?
OATES: I told you not to call me that!

> *They march on.*

SCOTT: Never had such pulling, all the time the sledge rasps and creaks. [*Calling*] Can we keep this up?
WILSON: I'm doing fine.
SCOTT: January tenth, we struggle to make good mileage over a dismal surface of blown crystals. [*Calling*] Our bodies will break, men.
WILSON: I find it quite invigorating.
SCOTT: I pull so hard I feel crushed inside.
WILSON: It's just lovely to be alive.
SCOTT: Each breath is a sword-swallowing exercise.

WILSON: Lovely, lovely, lovely.
BOWERS: For God's sake, will you stop?
WILSON: I'm sorry, are you speaking to me?
BOWERS: Must you always be so affable?
WILSON: No, I suppose not.
BOWERS: Must you always agree?
WILSON: I'm sorry, you're absolutely right.
BOWERS: Apologise for every step you take?
WILSON: If I'm sorry, then I'll say I am. I can't imagine why you would have a problem with that.
BOWERS: I have a problem with women like you, full stop.
WILSON: Women like me?
BOWERS: What have you done? Where have you been? Do you ever have an opinion?
WILSON: You don't know me.
BOWERS: What's to know?
WILSON: I'll have you know I've lived a very full life.
BOWERS: Full of what?
WILSON: Full of very good things.
BOWERS: Yes?
WILSON: I've had a good marriage, four wonderful children.
BOWERS: So what?
WILSON: What do you mean, so what? That's a lot.
BOWERS: No, it's not. It's not enough.
WILSON: That's plenty.
BOWERS: What else? What else? You must have fit in more.
WILSON: I kept house. The family kept me busy.
BOWERS: Didn't your children grow up?
WILSON: Of course they did. I was involved in a lot of other things.
BOWERS: What? [*Pause.*] What?
WILSON: I don't know.
BOWERS: Did you waste your life?
WILSON: My family was my life.
BOWERS: Where are your husband and children now?

    Pause.

WILSON: I must have got too much for them. [*Accusing*] Where are yours?
BOWERS: Perhaps I never married, nor had children.

WILSON: Oh, I see.
BOWERS: What do you see?
WILSON: You're jealous of me.
SCOTT: I don't know what I should do if Wilson and Bowers weren't so determinedly cheerful.
BOWERS: I'm not jealous of you.
WILSON: It seems so.
BOWERS: We're both here, aren't we? Alone, in this miserable place, trying to survive. But you, you've had all the time in the world and done nothing with it.
WILSON: What did you want me to do?
BOWERS: Do a million things, be committed to something, be full of desires, plans, great designs.
WILSON: I've never had a sense of the world beyond me.
BOWERS: You had all this time.
WILSON: I didn't know how to turn things round.
BOWERS: Why not?
WILSON: I would have had to be defiant.
BOWERS: Yes, that's right.
WILSON: There's no way I could be. It was bred out of me.
BOWERS: [*suddenly weeping*] All that time. All that time.
SCOTT: January fifteenth, we set off in high spirits, on the verge of triumph. Two long marches will land us at the Pole. Lengthen your strides, lads, we'll soon be raising our glasses.
EVANS: Who's he to tell us what to do? Who gave him the right? We're not here to take his orders. We don't have to put up with it, not at this stage of our lives. Find some fight, will you, for Christ's sakes? Find some fight.
OATES: I'm buggered, I don't mind telling you.

> EVANS *throws his questions at* SCOTT *who is focused on the images he sees before him.*

EVANS: Did you hear him? We're exhausted.
BOWERS: I'd like to rest.
EVANS: Are you deaf?
WILSON: I don't mind going on a little longer.

> BOWERS *groans at* WILSON*'s affability.*

But I'm actually very tired.

EVANS: We're all exhausted, bugger you.
SCOTT: The Norwegians must either be behind us or have suffered a mishap that has forced them to turn back. Otherwise where are their tracks? Pull, pull, let us be first to put our flag up.
EVANS: He's deaf to our complaints, blind and dumb, too. He's a heartless bastard who needs to be told a thing or two.
SCOTT: In two short days we will become the first human beings to reach the South Pole.
OATES: My feet hurt.
WILSON: My bunions ache.
BOWERS: I want to go inside.
OATES: I need a whisky. No ice.
EVANS: We've had enough of you telling us what to do.
SCOTT: January sixteenth, we march a good seven and a half miles. Tomorrow will see us at our destination.
EVANS: I'll report you; I'll tell them you're deranged, that's what I'll do.
SCOTT: On a long downhill stretch and under a cloudless sky, we see mock suns with great horizontal halos. Keep going, men, we're doing well.
OATES: I've had enough.
BOWERS: I can't go on.
WILSON: Nor can I.
EVANS: We refuse to take another step.

The four trekkers stop. SCOTT *suddenly lets out a haunting cry.*

SCOTT: [*in despair*] Look, men, look. Is that a cairn ahead?

Despite themselves, his fellow trekkers look.

My heart feels an awful tug of dread. With our hearts in our mouths, and not daring to hope, we go on, all eyes fixed on the dreaded object ahead. [*He marches on alone.*] The cairn coalesced into a black speck and then, smashing all hopes and dreams, into the blackest of black flags. [*Devastated*] The Norwegians have forestalled us and are first at the Pole.

END OF ACT ONE

ACT TWO

SCENE ONE

In the distance there appears a shape, like a cairn, holding a black flag on a pole. The light is sallow. It is terribly cold.

MARIA, *in the elegant gown of a diva, her feet bare on the ice, sings.*

Song: 'Solveig's Song'—Edward Grieg *(from* Peer Gynt*).*

SCOTT *traverses the ice. Curled in on himself, he looks a smaller man. He walks with heavy, laboured steps.*

MARIA *finishes her song and takes the black flag, which is actually a shawl, and puts it around her shoulders. She exits.*

SCOTT: Well, we have turned our back on the goal of our ambition and must face our eight hundred miles of solid dragging—and goodbye to most of the daydreams! The weight of my heart makes miserable bearing, yet I am forced to drag it, heavy and broken, back to base. My men have witnessed their leader revealed a snivelling failure. Leader! What kind of leader takes men as powerful, as honest and true as these, and risks their lives for a folly? How will I meet their eye, share the confines of our tent? How shall I bear the pity that will pour like treacle in sticky tones? How will I find the strength to return, a man who comes in second best on the breath of someone else's success? I shudder at the thought of the jeers from the disappointed ordinary men and women in the street who had taken each step with me towards the Pole. [*He suddenly looks very old, uneasy on his feet.*] I'm a fake. I've ventured no further than a book, travelled nowhere beyond the route my fingertip took as it traced its way along the lines of a map.

    WILSON *enters and observes* SCOTT.

WILSON: You look cold, Scot. Perhaps I'll get you a jacket from inside.
SCOTT: It has turned a little chilly.
WILSON: You look tired, Scot.
SCOTT: I could do with a bit of a lie-down.

WILSON: Just stay put for a while, have a cup of tea and perhaps some scones and jam.
SCOTT: Yes, that's a fine idea.
WILSON: You push yourself too far, Scot.
SCOTT: Not far enough, it seems.
WILSON: Was it a race?
SCOTT: I don't know what it was.
WILSON: Surely the experience has been great.
SCOTT: If not somewhat marred by my failure.
WILSON: You a failure? No, that's not you.
SCOTT: I should have made more of my life.
WILSON: You did what you could.
SCOTT: [*whispering*] I did not fulfil a single dream.

He weeps.

WILSON: Oh, Scot, in all these years, you have never shown me this side of you.
SCOTT: What kind of man am I now to burden you?
WILSON: But can't you see it's no burden? It's a pleasure that finally you allow me in.
SCOTT: Into this nightmare?
WILSON: Dream or nightmare, I don't care. To have something to talk through, about our fears, our hopes, good or bad, to talk closely is all I've ever wanted to do.
SCOTT: I never intentionally kept you out. I've been a solitary man. I saw it as my responsibility to grapple with my own doubts.

He drops his head into his hands and retreats into himself.

WILSON: When our Anne lost her sight and we had to wait to see if the operation was a success, and Brendan lost his job and for so long he couldn't find another and he seemed low, desperately low, and when your mother died and she'd meant so much to you, and to me as well, you said nothing. You never once confided in me, talked to me, shared the grief.
SCOTT: I'm not a man to express my feelings well.
WILSON: Once I miscarried, but I couldn't tell you. I lay in bed and pretended I had the flu. I was too afraid you wouldn't be able to say anything, or hear me say anything to you.

SCOTT: I wish with all my heart that I could make it up to you.
WILSON: I'm sure you could.
SCOTT: Because I have all the time for you. You mean everything to me, you are a steadfast and true friend, and I…
WILSON: Love me? Do you? Do you love me?
SCOTT: I do. I love you.
WILSON: I have always felt that you have not.
SCOTT: The moment I saw you come through the door, I loved you.
WILSON: You have not loved me deeply.
SCOTT: As deep as the chasms in the snow that take an entire sled and no sound is heard below.
WILSON: You have never touched me, really touched me.
SCOTT: I can touch you now.
WILSON: An embrace will not do.
SCOTT: I will cover you in kisses from head to toe.
WILSON: And more. Much more is needed.
SCOTT: Whatever you require.
WILSON: I require you to devour me.
SCOTT: Devour you?
WILSON: With great ardour.
SCOTT: I am grateful for the chance.
WILSON: I want you to take great pleasure in it.
SCOTT: Not a problem at all.
WILSON: I will take great pleasure myself.
SCOTT: Right. Good.
WILSON: You're not to be shocked.
SCOTT: No, I promise, I will not.
WILSON: If you are, you must hide it.
SCOTT: I will not be shocked.
WILSON: Good. Let's begin.

  SCOTT *and* WILSON *passionately embrace.*

SCENE TWO

The three trekkers, OATES, BOWERS *and* EVANS, *huddle together.*

OATES: I'm not well.
BOWERS: I'm not well.

EVANS: I'm not well.

　　WILSON *joins them.*

WILSON: [*exultant*] I'm utterly exhausted.

　　SCOTT *enters and addresses his men.*

SCOTT: For a moment there I was in total despair. I lost sight completely of my endeavour. But thanks to Wilson here, I'm back, raring to go as ever.

OATES: Oh no, I'm really not well.

BOWERS: Not at all well.

EVANS: No, not well.

WILSON: I'm as tired as hell.

SCOTT: You are men of great strength. Your fortitude puts me in awe. You have given me everything I could have asked for. Loyalty, commitment, dedication, and with a stoicism that belongs to a bygone age.

BOWERS: My tummy's upset.

OATES: I'm about to retch.

EVANS: Something burning right here.

WILSON: I've got some very tender bits.

EVANS: My gut's fucked.

OATES: Keep it clean.

SCOTT: Altitude problems, severe headaches, nosebleeds, and oxygen shortage have not daunted you.

BOWERS: I've a pain…

EVANS: In my neck.

OATES: In my feet.

BOWERS: In my knees.

WILSON: In my… never you mind.

SCOTT: Dehydration caused by increased respiration has put us under enormous strain, but there's been no stopping you.

OATES: And here.

EVANS: Here.

BOWERS: Here.

WILSON: And here.

SCOTT: We've had our fingers nipped, inch-long blisters filled with frozen liquid; and our noses and lips split. We've endured our afflictions as one.

OATES: My heart…

EVANS: My head…
BOWERS: My face…
WILSON: My entire body…
ALL: Aches.
SCOTT: Endless hours, days, weeks, months of man-hauling have taken their toll.
WILSON: I've got cystitis—Honeymoon Disease, they call it.
OATES: I've got gout, for God's sake.
EVANS: I've got arthritis.
WILSON: I've got osteoporosis.
BOWERS: I've got gingivitis.
WILSON: I've a peptic ulcer.
OATES: I've septicaemia.
WILSON: My tongue's irritated.
BOWERS: I've anaemia.
WILSON: I suffer from breathlessness.
OATES: I've angina.
EVANS: I have anxiety attacks.
BOWERS: I have that.
OATES: I've lumps.
EVANS: I'll give you lumps.
OATES: I've sores that won't heal.
WILSON: I've dermatitis—between my fingers here.
BOWERS: Itch, I itch all over.
OATES: Like ants crawling. It gives me the creeps.
EVANS: I'm constipated.

They moan in agreement.

SCOTT: I must ask you now to dig deep, to find the strength to endure it all again and make our way home.
WILSON: I haven't been in so long.
OATES: I have terrible trouble getting it out.
BOWERS: It's the food. It binds you.
EVANS: I miss having a good shit.

They moan in agreement.

SCOTT: No, we were not first at the Pole. But we were there, we made it, we got there and honourably so.

OATES: I've survived three operations.
EVANS: Five.
WILSON: I've had four children and I was under for every one—that must count. And I've had two others, more serious, so that's six in all.
BOWERS: I've got a scar here on my side. I must have had my appendix out.
OATES: I've had my hips done. Terrible mess they made of it. I went in for the one and got something golden and it had to be redone.
EVANS: My heart's been out beating in a dish beside me. Five valves fixed.
OATES: With my second one, I lost a lot of blood.
EVANS: I lost a lot of blood.
OATES: I lost a ton.
WILSON: I had none. When I had all my bits scraped out. Not a scrap left. Whish! All gone.
EVANS: I've had my prostate done.

    BOWERS *gasps and feels her breasts.*

BOWERS: I thought perhaps I might have…
SCOTT: I ask you to put your faith in me one more time and I will reward your trust and lead us home.
OATES: Fortunately my mind is as good as gold.
BOWERS: As is mine.
EVANS: I'm as sharp as a tack.
BOWERS: And me. I'm sharp. I'm as sharp as… that.
WILSON: No trouble in that department.
BOWERS: Nor me. None. Not at all. No.

    SCOTT *makes a move forward and stops.*

SCOTT: There's no sign of the track. Keep your eyes glued, men, if we miss our depots the consequences will be fatal. Fan out.

    They exit in all directions.

SCENE THREE

BOWERS *and* WILSON *enter from opposite directions.*

BOWERS: I know exactly where I am.
WILSON: Of course you do.

BOWERS: I tell you I do.
WILSON: You don't have to tell me.
BOWERS: How dare you suggest I've lost my way.
WILSON: I would never suggest any such thing. You look like someone who knows exactly where she is.
BOWERS: For Christ's sake, I do, I do know. I don't just look as if I do, I do, I actually do. It's you who hasn't a clue.
WILSON: That's quite likely. Yes, it's true, I don't. Where are we?
BOWERS: There you go, asking silly questions.
WILSON: I don't care where I am. I don't care about anything. I could take all my clothes off.
BOWERS: Please, don't do that.
WILSON: I could take all my clothes off, and… go stand in the middle of the street.
BOWERS: Don't.
WILSON: I could say to all the motorists, feast your eyes on me.
BOWERS: Why would you want to do that?
WILSON: I feel so tingly, so wonderfully tingly all over.
BOWERS: Keep those sorts of things to yourself.
WILSON: I want to tell the world I'm in love.
BOWERS: A little modesty isn't a bad thing.
WILSON: I've lost all inhibition. All gone.
BOWERS: Well, find it again.
WILSON: Why stop yourself feeling pleasure? Enormous pleasure.
BOWERS: Oh, please.
WILSON: Have you ever been in love?
BOWERS: Everyone's been in love.
WILSON: So in love that you want to give every bit of yourself?
BOWERS: Yes, I probably have.
WILSON: That you just want to let yourself go, entirely go?
BOWERS: Probably.
WILSON: Don't you know?
BOWERS: Yes, I know. Of course I bloody know. I just said so, didn't I?
WILSON: And I've never felt so loved. So completely loved. Have you ever been completely loved?
BOWERS: I'm sure I have. I'm certain I have.
WILSON: I've never had my body loved so utterly.

BOWERS: Well, I have, I know I have. I bloody have, so shut up about it.
WILSON: Have you ever heard of multiple orgasms?
BOWERS: How dare you keep asking me these ridiculous questions?
WILSON: And the G-spot?
BOWERS: I want you to stop.
WILSON: I seem to have lost all sense of decorum.
BOWERS: I don't have to tell you anything about myself.
WILSON: I think I might at least take off my dress.
BOWERS: I've loved, and been loved. Lots. Lots and lots of love.
WILSON: I might take it all off.

> BOWERS *has had enough and runs away from* WILSON.

Perhaps I might do a little dance.

> WILSON *does a wild little dance and shrieks with joy and happily wanders off.*

> EVANS *and* OATES *enter from different directions.* OATES *sees* EVANS *and turns to leave.*

EVANS: Ah, just the man I wanted to see.

> OATES *reluctantly turns to face* EVANS.

OATES: I'm in a bit of a hurry, actually, I'm looking for…
EVANS: What have you lost?
OATES: Ah… my dog.
EVANS: Let's walk together, shall we? We might cross his path. I miss a good talk every now and then, you know, one on one, between men.
OATES: That's not my forte, I'm afraid, talk between men. I've never known what to say. I like the idea of it, I like it a great deal. Like father and son talks, I like the idea of them, I thought that would be a good thing to do, to meander about, perhaps in a shed, putting something together, building something, a fence maybe, or a brick wall. Where you've got your eyes on the task, none of this intense eye-to-eye I'm talking to you, just doing your business and you chat, on and off, you chat and there's silence and you say functional things, too, like hand me the glue, or the hammer, or hold this bit of wire, would you? And things get said, about bits that might be worrying you, like something someone has said, or the amount of work you've got hanging over your head. And you might say

something about what you like, and what you don't like. You might reveal things to each other and things might be said that puts whatever is niggling at you in a different light. Suddenly it might seem trivial and silly and nothing at all to worry about. But like I said, I never got into the swing of talking. My father had no skill at it, I can tell you. And me, I guess I never learnt to do it, either. I wish I could have learned. I dearly wish I could.

EVANS: There are those who think I say too much, that I should keep my big mouth shut. I've never been one to remain quiet. If the things that mean something to me are under attack I speak out. Remain silent, and essential things, things that are at the heart of you, will be lost. Like ideals.

OATES: Oh yes, ideals. I used to think they were important.

EVANS: Ideals are worth the fight. Ideals are what make us constantly seek a better life.

OATES: Now I'm not so certain.

EVANS: Without them we're lost.

OATES: They lead to disaster.

EVANS: You have to speak up loud and clear for your ideals or they'll be quashed.

A mournful howl echoes in the distance.

OATES: I've got to find my dog.

OATES *exits.* EVANS *doesn't notice. An agitated* BOWERS *enters.* EVANS *fails to recognise he is talking to someone else.*

EVANS: Oh no, I've never been at a loss for words. It's something I've always been good at, words, always had a way with them. I amaze myself at how easily they flow. They soar and dip and lift like a score for an orchestra.

BOWERS: Good for you.

EVANS: They are a powerful weapon, words.

BOWERS: They do nothing but betray me.

EVANS: They've held me in awe.

BOWERS: They are treacherous things.

EVANS: They've brought me to tears, struck at my very core.

BOWERS: They rush off and leave me stranded.

EVANS: And when they tell the truth, they're formidable things.

BOWERS: I don't want the truth. Take the truth and shove it.
EVANS: You don't know what you're saying. The truth keeps you from going mad.
BOWERS: The truth is utterly sad.
EVANS: Truth's a mighty thing. It shatters bullshit with a single blow.
BOWERS: Truth's a slippery eel.
EVANS: It hits like a lightning strike, it lifts the lid off hell and frees the damned.
BOWERS: It's nothing but cruel.
EVANS: I'm a godless man, but I believe the truth can cleanse the soul.
BOWERS: Cruel.
EVANS: It turns despair around, it allows one to start anew.
BOWERS: I sat face to face with a man I didn't know. In one hand, I held a page of questions, in the other, a microphone. We sat in silence. Finally he lifted his eyebrow. And his lip. It curled. He asked me my name. [*Pause.*] I said, I will not say who I am, I'll keep my name to myself, thank you very much, my name's my name and I will not be asked these silly questions. I will not. [*Pause.*] I never interviewed anyone again. [*Pause.*] The truth is I don't know where I am. The truth is I don't know who I am.
EVANS: We have to fight, that's the truth.
BOWERS: I'm of no use.
EVANS: We deserve a better life.
BOWERS: There's no better life to be had.
EVANS: Fight for justice.
BOWERS: There's been none of that for years.
EVANS: Equality.
BOWERS: Nor that.
EVANS: For humanity.
BOWERS: Those things are old hat. The truth is, time has run out.

> EVANS *is most disconcerted.*

What, no words?

> BOWERS *turns and exits.* EVANS *exits in the opposite direction.*

> MARIA *enters. Forlornly, she turns in circles.*

MARIA: I'm lost. I'm lost. I'm lost.

> SCOTT *enters.*

SCOTT: Is this some sort of snow blindness I am suffering? Hallucinations out here are quite conceivable. But a weeping woman on the ice!

He approaches the circling MARIA *and when she sees him she stops.*

It will be alright.
MARIA: It will not.
SCOTT: You're safe now.
MARIA: I am lost.
SCOTT: I've found you. Don't cry.
MARIA: I am inconsolable.
SCOTT: Come now, we'll soon have things fixed.
MARIA: My home no longer exists.
SCOTT: You'll see your country in no time.
MARIA: My country has been stolen from me.
SCOTT: You must be one of Amundsen's team.
MARIA: I don't play sport.
SCOTT: A Norskie who has been left behind.
MARIA: I've been searching for my country for so long now, but the landscape never changes. It's always the same.
SCOTT: It's a miracle that I crossed your path. Congratulations, you must be very proud.
MARIA: Proud? Of what?
SCOTT: To be the first to hoist your country's flag.
MARIA: I'm not proud of flags. The town where I was born is populated by strangers, by those who speak a different language, who pray to a different god. My country hoisted its flag and another country pulled it down.
SCOTT: You have traversed a new and undiscovered land.
MARIA: What's to discover?
SCOTT: Through discovery great advancements are made.
MARIA: And dreams are trodden on.
SCOTT: It's human nature to desire to know what's beyond.
MARIA: Why can't you tolerate mystery?
SCOTT: You're delirious, Norskie.
MARIA: And you're deluded. You believe in an heroic age.
SCOTT: I do.
MARIA: You're a romantic fool.

SCOTT: I'll take you home.
MARIA: I used to shower with my grandmamma. Her breast would rest on the top of my head like a snug cap. She'd sing at the top of her voice and I would join her in the chorus. My only comfort is to imagine the warm water trickling down my arms and legs.
SCOTT: You'll be right again.
MARIA: No, I will not.

She turns to exit.

SCOTT: Wait! You're doomed if you venture out there alone.

She turns.

MARIA: I know.

MARIA *exits.*

SCENE FOUR

A bewildered BOWERS *enters.*

SCOTT: Good man, Birdie! You've found the track.
BOWERS: Birdie?
SCOTT: Ahoy, lads! We're on our way.

A makeshift sail, closely resembling a white bedsheet, billows out in a sudden wind. OATES, EVANS *and a beaming* WILSON *enter and join* SCOTT *and* BOWERS.

The southerly is strong and the tent floor serves us well to sail our sledge across the sand-like crystals which make man-hauling hell.

He assesses his team. They stand beside him, off in their own worlds. OATES *lifts his head and whistles for his creature.*

Oates is somewhat distracted but is holding his own.

WILSON *hugs herself and giggles with pleasure.*

Wilson is unable to continue his rock collection, but nevertheless his spirits remain high. And Birdie…
BOWERS: Yes, that's me. Is it?
SCOTT: … is as strong as ever.
BOWERS: [*pointing in different directions*] This way. This way.
SCOTT: But Evans…

EVANS *warms his hands beneath his armpits.*

EVANS: I feel the cold creeping over my collar and down my neck.
SCOTT: Evans' hands have deteriorated further.
EVANS: Seeping in through my flesh.
SCOTT: The last thing you need is one of your team holding you up.
EVANS: Into my bones. I will not be warm again.
SCOTT: There is no doubt Evans is a good deal run-down.
EVANS: Truth is uncovering me. Taking off my overcoat and leaving me exposed.
SCOTT: He is very much annoyed with himself, which is not a good sign.
EVANS: A snivelling, feeble, old man, with no flesh on my bones, put out on the ice.
SCOTT: To my surprise he shows signs of losing heart.
EVANS: All the heat in me leaking out.
SCOTT: It's with some urgency, men, that I tell you time is running out. Let's step long and fast.

The sail billows out. They march. EVANS *lags behind.*

BOWERS: This way. This way.
SCOTT: Every moment is an effort in the face of the ceaseless wind.
EVANS: This is not how it was meant to be.
SCOTT: Death awaits us if we fail. March, men, march, we must prevail.
EVANS: Glorious days are what I imagined.
SCOTT: Two days only of rations on the sledge.
EVANS: A grand world with a grand future is what I'd see.
SCOTT: Twenty-five miles to our food cache and my intuition deserts me.
EVANS: I thought we'd achieve something great.
SCOTT: A labyrinth of ice towers and crevasses surround us. For God's sake, men, keep together. We descend into an icy version of hell.

They stop and stand in silence. A labyrinth of ice towers and crevasses surround them.

SCENE FIVE

SCOTT *is inside the labyrinth.*

SCOTT: Stay close, men, this is a place where demons lurk. [*He turns to find he's alone.*] Men? Men!

SCOTT *exits.*

BOWERS *enters. She is disorientated.*

ALEX *can be heard calling 'Claudia'. The calls are distorted and strange in the echoing chambers of the ice.*

BOWERS: A table, a chair, a bed, a quilt, a tray, a plate, a knife and fork, and spoon, a serviette, a glass, a cup, a teaspoon. I'm alright. Curtains, linoleum, flowers, carnations, in a vase, on the bedside table. Window, door, doorknob, opens onto a… corridor. [*Referring to the word*] Ah, I got you.

ALEX *finally appears.*

ALEX: Claudia!

For an exquisite second BOWERS *recognises her name.*

BOWERS: Yes.

And then forgets it. She disappears down an ice tunnel. ALEX *disappears down another.*

SCOTT *emerges from a crevasse.*

SCOTT: Wilson, Bowers, Evans, Oates? I'm Theseus in the maze in desperate need of Ariadne and her ball of thread. If I come face to face with a Minotaur I know then that I've indeed come to the end.

As SCOTT *disappears down a crevasse, the* CREATURE *appears. It howls eerily.* OATES *appears a moment later.*

OATES: Where are you, creature? [*He sees the* CREATURE *and is greatly relieved.*] I miss you, boy. I miss you so much.

The CREATURE *disappears down a tunnel.*

Wait!

MARIA *enters as* OATES *exits to pursue the* CREATURE. *She calls after him.*

MARIA: I've been looking for the door. Excuse me, could you help me find the door?!

MARIA *exits.* WILSON *appears from a crevasse.* SCOTT *appears from another and they collide.*

SCOTT: Wilson. Thank God.

WILSON: I've been searching for you everywhere, Scot.
SCOTT: We've found each other, my dear friend.
WILSON: I'm about to burst out of my skin. Quick, while we've got the chance.

She pulls down her trousers. SCOTT *realises her intention and immediately pulls his trousers down also.* WILSON *draws him into a tunnel.*

The CREATURE *rushes out of an ice tunnel with an exhausted* OATES *close on his heels. The* CREATURE *stops suddenly at what seems to be a dead end.*

OATES: Got you at last, my dear, dear boy.

The CREATURE *looks up and a large dead tree looms above him.* OATES *follows his gaze and is devastated.*

Oh no, no, no.

The CREATURE *begins to climb the tree.* OATES *falls to his knees and weeps pitifully. The* CREATURE *sits in the tree and lets out a most mournful howl.* OATES *and the* CREATURE *and the tree disappear in the darkness.*

EVANS *enters from a tunnel.*

EVANS: Lost. Utterly lost. I wanted to change the fucking world! Do you stand by and watch a man be beaten to a pulp, do you close your ears to his cries for help? No. You pull the assailant off, you oppose the thuggery, you fight. Lost. To a world that protects the few. I gave up my life for a party that would fight for what's decent and right. But it gave up virtue for dirty deals, gave up principles for unscrupulous acts, and gave up the very reason for its existence. Where's the resistance, the struggle, our persistence? Lost. Resistance? Struggle? Even these words I use. Lost.

EVANS *disappears down a crevasse.*

SCENE SIX

On the open plain, SCOTT, WILSON, BOWERS *and* OATES *stand in a line.*

SCOTT: Taff Evans has collapsed numerous times, sick and giddy and unable to walk. He has nearly broken down in brain I think and is

absolutely changed from his normal self-reliant self. He's out of the sledge traces and plods along in our tracks. [*He calls out to* EVANS, *thinking he is behind him.*] How goes it, Evans?! [*He looks back to see that* EVANS *is nowhere to be seen.*] Evans!
WILSON: We've lost him, I'm afraid.
BOWERS: Who?
OATES: Last saw him when we crossed at the lights.
SCOTT: Evans!

> EVANS *appears on his hands and knees in an icy light. The light gradually dims.*

SCENE SEVEN

SCOTT, BOWERS, OATES *and* WILSON *form a funereal line.*

SCOTT: It's a terrible thing to lose a companion in this way.
WILSON: A terrible thing.
OATES: Shocking.
WILSON: We'll miss him.
BOWERS: Who?
OATES: He's out of his misery now, that's the thing.
SCOTT: What a desperate pass we were in with a sick man on our hands and at such a distance from home.
WILSON: It's often the most powerful of men who die quickly.
OATES: I'm amazed he died before me.
WILSON: I've outlived so many.
OATES: And me. I'd give my right arm to be taken, right here, right now.
SCOTT: I'll miss the heat of the man dearly.
OATES: It's not right to live longer than your young.
WILSON: You can't choose, can you?
OATES: No.
WILSON: You can't say, excuse me, take me…
OATES: No.
WILSON: … it's me who should have died.
BOWERS: Who died?
SCOTT: Taff Evans, the biggest, heaviest and most muscular man in the party.
BOWERS: Too bad.

SCOTT: We struggle for every breath. Whatever compassion we have left is for ourselves.
WILSON: I'd like to be missed when I go.
OATES: By someone. Your child. Your son.
WILSON: By a loved one.
BOWERS: [*vague*] This way. This way.
WILSON: It's only a matter of time.
OATES: Indeed.
SCOTT: Come, men, we've one member gone, but we needn't feel we must join him. We must get back before winter sets in and locks us up in ice. [*He searches the horizon.*] Only four hundred miles with a comparatively light sledgeload. Survival is within our grasp.
BOWERS: This way. This way.

SCENE EIGHT

OATES *appears, carrying the* CREATURE *on his back. He trudges slowly and with great effort. He breathes laboriously.*

CREATURE: A two-headed giant, we are.
OATES: We are indeed.
CREATURE: My hands are warm in your beard.
OATES: Hold on tight.
CREATURE: Have we far to go?
OATES: As far as you like.
CREATURE: I can see above the clouds.
OATES: Can you now?
CREATURE: I can look down on the world.
OATES: You show me the way.
CREATURE: It's a wondrous place.
OATES: Oh, my dear boy.
CREATURE: I'm heavy, aren't I?
OATES: You're light.
CREATURE: Are you tired?
OATES: You'll keep me awake.
CREATURE: You won't drop me?
OATES: No, lad, I've stitched you on.
CREATURE: I might fall.

OATES: I'll catch you.
CREATURE: I might slip from your grasp.
OATES: I won't let you.
CREATURE: And fall on my arse.

They laugh.

OATES: You're safe with me, boy, I promise you.

The CREATURE *howls mightily.*

SCENE NINE

SCOTT, OATES, BOWERS *and* WILSON *hang in their sleeping bags. A sleeping body hangs in Evans' bag. They are buffeted by the raging wind.*

SCOTT: A blizzard has struck and the temperature has plunged with a vengeance. From February twenty-fifth onwards our thermometer recorded minus twenty, from February twenty-seventh, it recorded minus thirty, and only five days later, minus forty. The blue skies have clouded over, dark and forbidding, and worst of all, Oates announced that his feet were in a bad state. I should have known; for days he's walked as if he's carrying an extra load.

OATES suddenly howls in pain.

He suffers the pains of hell every time his feet thaw out.

WILSON waves a bad smell away from her nose.

WILSON: Pooh!
SCOTT: The stench of rotting flesh overwhelms us.
WILSON: Whoever's responsible for that smell, please go outside.
SCOTT: Poor Soldier has become a terrible hindrance.

OATES howls.

WILSON: Stop that confounded noise!
OATES: [*calling out*] Forgive me, boy, they won't let me bring you inside.
SCOTT: One feels for Oates the crisis is near.

The body in Evan's bag stirs. It's MARIA.

WILSON: What's she doing here?
SCOTT: You see her? I thought perhaps she was some daft thing from my mind.

WILSON: She's always getting into other people's beds. I've told her but she refuses to sleep in her own.

    MARIA *is awake, but still appears asleep.*

MARIA: I have no bed here.

WILSON: Of course you do.

MARIA: No thank you, I do not intend to stay long.

SCOTT: The blizzard's been raging for days. You may find you're here for quite some time.

MARIA: I am leaving very soon.

WILSON: Where to?

SCOTT: We're stuck here, I'm afraid.

MARIA: I don't belong here.

WILSON: Here she goes.

SCOTT: The cold, the shortage of food and the strain is beginning to derange us all.

    OATES *howls.*

Watching one another perish inch by inch might take many nightmare days and nights. I desperately hope to hear the dogs sent out from Cape Evans to meet us.

    OATES *howls.*

I cannot bear Soldier's misery much longer. Wilson, it's time.

WILSON: For love, my dear Scot?

SCOTT: There are enough opiate tablets in the medical box to provide each man with a quick way out.

WILSON: A quick way out?

SCOTT: Distribute the tablets, Wilson. The decision to die must be put in each of our hands.

WILSON: You want to die, Scot?

SCOTT: We all must have the choice.

WILSON: I choose to fight for every breath.

SCOTT: To have the means of ending our troubles in your pocket may prove an odd comfort.

WILSON: It's not right, Scot, to interrupt life, not even one's own. God only can take on that responsibility.

    OATES *howls miserably.*

SCOTT: Can you hear that, Wilson? How much misery must one man endure?
WILSON: Some things are beyond us, Scot. Things happen because they're meant to. Like me and you: we're meant to see each other through.
SCOTT: I see it's difficult for you, Wilson, but to allow such misery is plainly cruel.

> OATES *howls.*

Soldier, you have fought long and hard, make it a little easier on yourself.
OATES: I thought there was no better way than to never wake from sleep, but now I'm desperate to feel death's every blow.
SCOTT: The pain must be unbearable.
OATES: It never ebbs. I've lived with it a long time. It'll stay with me to the end.
MARIA: I've lined up pills, stood on railway tracks, sat in a warm bath with my best kitchen knife, but I'm programmed to survive, it's all I know to do.
SCOTT: [*to* BOWERS] And Birdie? What about you?

> BOWERS *stares out, her brain gone.*

Birdie? Bowers?

> BOWERS *stares.*

[*Sadly*] For Birdie, the offer has come too late.
WILSON: And you, Scott?
SCOTT: I despair, I hope, I despair. Life is a multifarious collection of feelings but we rarely experience its extremes. I'm too interested in the journey to cut it short. [*Pause.*] And I couldn't bear to leave you.

> OATES *climbs out of his sleeping bag.*

OATES: Do not go gentle into that good night,
　　Old age should burn and rave at close of day;
　　Rage, rage against the dying of the light.
SCOTT: What are you doing, Oates?
OATES: I am just going outside and may be some time.

> OATES *exits. The others hang in silence.*

SCENE TEN

OATES *is on the ice. The* CREATURE *has gone and in his stead stands* PETER. *He wears the military uniform of an Australian soldier in Vietnam.*

OATES: Have we time?
PETER: Some.
OATES: I didn't expect to see you in uniform.
PETER: I thought it'd please you.
OATES: Please me? No.
PETER: Once it pleased you.
OATES: Once.
PETER: You were as proud as Punch.
OATES: I was.
PETER: Look at my son!
OATES: That's right.
PETER: It didn't last.
OATES: I was always proud of you.
PETER: Not when I came home.
OATES: I didn't understand.
PETER: I heard you in the kitchen once talking to Mum. You called me a weak prick.
OATES: I said that?
PETER: You did. You saw me cry. All of us cried, in our beers, in the arms of our wives. We'd laugh and out would pour tears.
OATES: I couldn't handle your misery.
PETER: You were ashamed of me.
OATES: I knew what you must have been through.
PETER: You never asked.
OATES: You served your country in Vietnam. There was nothing wrong with that.
PETER: I shouldn't have gone.
OATES: War's tough, that's all.
PETER: What do you know about war?
OATES: Nothing.
PETER: Not a thing.
OATES: I thought it was something you had to do.

PETER: Who, me? Or you?
OATES: I would have gone, if I'd had the chance.
PETER: Lucky me. I get to fight someone else's war.
OATES: Where's this heading?
PETER: You know exactly where it's heading.

Pause.

OATES: There must've been something worth living for.
PETER: Living hurt.
OATES: You could've called someone.
PETER: I called.
OATES: I didn't hear.
PETER: No.
OATES: You're fucking cruel.

PETER *laughs.*

Did you ever think of anyone else? Did you ever think of me?
PETER: I thought it'd be a relief to you.
OATES: You weak prick.

PETER *growls quietly, creature-like.*

What are you made of?
PETER: [*growling*] Here we go.
OATES: You think you had it tough. Jesus Christ, others have done it and come out alright. Others made it through. Held on tight.
PETER: This weak prick didn't.
OATES: No.
PETER: A noise and I'd shriek. Someone would touch me and I'd jump out of my skin. I'd mislay my keys and I'd start snivelling.
OATES: You could've done something about it.
PETER: Like what?
OATES: You could've called someone.
PETER: I called.
OATES: I didn't hear.
PETER: No.
OATES: You're fucking cruel.

PETER *laughs.*

There were others who went. They don't milk it the way you do.

PETER *growls.*

They got on with their lives.

PETER: Couldn't keep their jobs or their wives, hit the piss, got constantly sick. They're weak pricks too.

OATES: You could've—

PETER: I called!

Pause. PETER *howls, creature-like, turns and walks away.*

OATES: [*alarmed*] I hear you now, Peter. I hear you.

PETER *turns to* OATES *and looks sadly at his father.*

I think of you every day. I think of you… hanging from that tree.

PETER: I couldn't take it anymore.

OATES: It's not right to outlive your son.

PETER: It was agony.

OATES: Agony's what you've left me, I've missed you so.

PETER: I'm here now.

OATES: You are.

PETER: And it's time to go.

They take each other by the hand and walk across the ice.

SCENE ELEVEN

SCOTT *and* WILSON *are naked inside the one sleeping bag.*

WILSON: I've never felt happier in all my life than I feel right now.

SCOTT: To feel happy when the end draws near—we're indeed graced.

WILSON: I can barely believe I'm me.

SCOTT *gives* WILSON *a squeeze.*

SCOTT: You're you, alright.

WILSON *giggles.*

I yearned for a life of epic proportions and that's exactly what I got.

WILSON: You did, indeed.

SCOTT: We've experienced the greatest march ever made and come very near to great success.

WILSON: It's all because of you, Scot. You deserve to be remembered forever.

SCOTT: 'They died having done something great—how hard must not death be, having done nothing.' That's what someone will say about us one day.
WILSON: I'm so grateful that you included me in this wonderful and exciting journey.
SCOTT: We've been characters in a thrilling tale.
WILSON: Absolutely thrilling.
SCOTT: We've wrung every bit from life. Lived it—truly lived it. Not a bad time to die, Wilson.
WILSON: No, Scot, not bad at all.
SCOTT: One day our story, a splendid tragedy, will be told and we'll inspire millions to truly know the world, to love and respect it.
WILSON: What a good man you are, Scot.

> WILSON *kisses* SCOTT *tenderly.*
>
> *A man enters. He carries a bouquet of flowers. It is* SCOT, *Mary's husband.*

SCOT: Mary?

> WILSON *looks at him for some moments.*

For God's sake, what are you doing?
WILSON: Scot.
SCOT: Mary, please, what are you doing in bed with that man?
WILSON: Is that you, Scot?
SCOT: Of course it's me. I don't understand.
SCOTT: What is it, Wilson? Who is this man? Have we been saved?
WILSON: Oh, dear me.

> WILSON *lifts her hand to her mouth as she realises that she has confused her men. She looks at* SCOTT *and then at* SCOT *and then back at* SCOTT *again.*

SCOT: For God's sake, Mary, get up.
WILSON: It's been very cold, Scot.
SCOT: And get dressed.

> *She remembers that she's naked.*

WILSON: Oh, dear me.
SCOT: You're ridiculous.
SCOTT: Who is he?

WILSON: I'm a bit tired, Scot.
SCOT: Get up immediately.
WILSON: Perhaps you could visit some other time.
SCOT: I certainly will not. You stupid woman, you're making a fool of yourself.
WILSON: Don't talk to me like that.
SCOTT: Do you want me to tell him to shove off?
SCOT: She's my bloody wife.
SCOTT: Oh, I see. [*To* WILSON] Do you want me to tell him to shove off?
SCOT: I'm her husband.
WILSON: [*indicating* SCOTT] This man here is more husband to me.
SCOT: You've lost your mind, Mary.
WILSON: You abandoned me.
SCOT: I put you in here for your own good.
WILSON: Thank you, because it's in here I met the man of my dreams.
SCOT: Mary, come on, you don't know what you're doing. You're a little dreamy.
WILSON: Oh no, I don't think so.
SCOT: Come on, Mary, get out of the bed and we'll find your room.
WILSON: I'm comfortable.
SCOT: [*harshly*] I said, get up!

    WILSON *begins to lose her resolve.*

WILSON: I don't want to go.
SCOT: I haven't got time for this.
WILSON: Oh.
SCOT: Now.
WILSON: Why don't you leave me be?
SCOT: Come on, I said.
WILSON: Oh.
SCOT: Quick.

    WILSON *acquiesces.*

WILSON: I'm coming. Don't hurry me.
SCOTT: Don't go, Wilson.
SCOT: You stay out of it.
SCOTT: Wilson, stay with me.
SCOT: You've taken advantage of her enough.

SCOTT: Stay.
SCOT: Come on, Mary, I'll have everything fixed.
SCOTT: Wilson?
SCOT: Hurry up, damn you!
WILSON: [*to* SCOTT] Goodbye, my dear, dear Scott.

SCENE TWELVE

MARIA, *a diva, is wandering alone on the ice.*
She sings: 'Teneste la Promessa'— Giuseppe Verdi (from La Traviata*).*

SCENE THIRTEEN

SCOTT *is alone. He stands in his underwear. He seems a smaller man.*
MARIA *continues to sing.*

SCOTT: Wilson? Wilson, I want to tell you something before I go. Something I've been holding onto for quite some time. It seems silly now because I can't think why. [*Pause.*] I've never loved a woman before. Wilson, you are my first. My very, very first. [*Pause.*] Wilson? Bowers? Oates? Evans? My dear friends. We did something remarkable, didn't we, men?

The light slowly fades.

THE END

Ivan Donato (behind) as Joey and Greg Stone as Eric in the 2010 HotHouse Theatre production of THE BERRY MAN at the Butter Factory Theatre, Wodonga. (Photo: Karen Donnelly)

THE BERRY MAN

Ivan Donato as Joey and Greg Stone as Eric in the 2010 HotHouse Theatre production of THE BERRY MAN at the Butter Factory Theatre, Wodonga. (Photo: Karen Donnelly)

Introduction

It is such a great pleasure to work on a Patricia Cornelius play. She manages to capture 'humanity' in its most raw and fragile state because she is unafraid to tackle subjects that are taboo or 'difficult'. Her understanding of the human spirit cuts to the quick and she pulls no punches in the most poetic and poignant way. A deep thinker who wears her heart on her sleeve, she speaks her mind with candour and fluidity.

Patricia's father was a POW in Changi and she has always had a fascination with and interest in the experience of war. She spent months and months researching: devouring fiction and non-fiction books, going on field trips and interviewing a wide range of people associated with the Vietnam War. But she wasn't interested in writing another 'history play'. Instead she has captured, with humanity and empathy, the experiences of boys who go to war, and return as men. Most men who go to war come back 'changed', scarred and damaged in one way or another. *The Berry Man* delves into territory that too often gets ignored or put into the too-hard basket. It is a poignant and poetic work with a good dose of laughter thrown in.

Set in a harsh rural landscape, *The Berry Man* has two interwoven narratives.

In the first a man has inherited a farm. He is a stranger to the land and struggles to grow anything on it. As he tries, he conjures up—and is haunted by—the visitations from a young man. We see that until he deals with his past, of which the young man is a symbol, nothing will grow. The second narrative concerns a single woman who works her farm and is fiercely independent. But she yearns to have a baby and as she turns forty her maternal need intensifies. She becomes desperate for someone to make more than her garden grow.

The two narratives complement each other. They're both about fecundity, the giving of life, and an awareness of time running out. They revolve around loss, memory, grief, deeply personal secrets and the 'monkey' we carry on our backs.

The Berry Man was developed with HotHouse Theatre, and Playwriting Australia selected it as one of six plays to be workshopped and presented at the 2009 National Playwriting Festival in Hobart, Tasmania. When I was invited to direct the reading, it was not only a great opportunity to continue developing the play, but, as it turned out, it led to one of my most memorable nights in the theatre.

During the festival we worked intensely over a two-week period with a small group of actors and a dramaturge. The aim was to showcase the play as a moved reading over two nights at the Backspace Theatre behind the Theatre Royal.

After rehearsals and performances, the actors, playwrights, directors and dramaturges would gather at the Theatre Royal Hotel, next door to the theatre for a beer or two to unwind. So when we finished a technical rehearsal for *The Berry Man*, and wandered in for quiet ale, we noticed that the bar was much rowdier than usual. In fact it was filled mainly with men, all in their early sixties.

As the night drew to a close—and typically, our mob stayed till stumps—we noticed how these men were still holding up the bar, all in fine form and telling all sorts of tales. Patricia was the first to start chatting to them. In one of those great coincidences the group turned out to be Vietnam Vets. Not just any Vets but the The Vietnam Tunnel Rats. They had served as the Engineer Field Troops in Vietnam and went bush with the Armoured Corps and Infantry, often carrying out specialist duties such as mine and booby trap detection. They came from all around Australia and were staying at the hotel for their reunion: the fortieth anniversary of the Rats. So, some more beers were downed and more stories flowed; some funny, some terribly sad and poignant. Most of these men were getting on with their lives but they also had horrific tales to tell. It was a memorable night.

When the pub finally closed its doors, Patricia, with a rush of blood to the head, invited one of the men to our showcase performance the following evening (she said to me later that she secretly hoped he'd forget). Her invitee said he wasn't sure if he could make it anyway. There was an anniversary dawn march the next morning and it usually ended back at the pub afterwards for more reminiscing and drinking.

The National Playwriting Festival is really for industry people, industry peers and arts audiences. The plays presented are all brand new, with minimal staging and technical support, and most of the actors still have scripts in hands.

Lo and behold, an hour before the show the next day, out of the pub and along the laneway, came at least fifty of the Rats with their wives, heading for the theatre. Patricia had mentioned the reading to one of the wives the night before and apparently she'd organised the 'lot' to come. The image of this mob, our new-found friends, heading towards the theatre was a sight to behold! Patricia and I were not sure what to expect or, more to the point, what they were expecting. What did we say last night? Are they pissed? Have they ever seen a play reading before? Most of them had never even been to the theatre and would most likely be suspicious about what a playwright had to say about them.

I went backstage to let the actors know that 'The Rats and their wives' were in the house. A quick look of panic went around the dressing room, their terror and mine was palpable. Let's face it, this play is not a romantic or nostalgic piece that pays homage to our Diggers. It is a complex and brutal work about taboos, about being scared, about carrying secrets to the grave, about being left alone and hapless with no clue about how to fix yourself.

While Patricia and I were waiting in the foyer we got talking to one of the women who said the boys could react in three possible ways: they might get bored and walk out, they might get jittery and sing out things, or they might just watch.

By now it was 6.30 p.m. and the theatre bells were ringing. The house was pretty much full and one of the Rats was standing in the middle of the stage taking photos of his mates in the audience. The house lights went down. Chris Mead, the Artistic Director of Playwriting Australia, made a short speech, explaining what the night would entail and what a 'play reading' was.

Everyone was nervous, the Tunnel Rats, their wives, Patricia, myself, the actors and the rest of the audience. Patricia especially was shaking in her boots, unsure how these men would react to her material.

The Berry Man opens with a man standing motionless in the middle of a hoed paddock. He stands there for a very long time. The play spills out slowly, scene by scene, filled with confronting material about longing, about hidden secrets, ambiguous sexuality, pain, anger, grief, nightmares. One of the Rats shuffled and made his way out. Shortly after he returned—it was only a toilet stop. In the first ten minutes there were some giggles and whispers but by the end of the play there was silence—absolute silence—and attention.

The play finished. There was a moment when the silence in the theatre felt enormous, and then, with great relief, the audience broke into loud applause. Many of the men were wiping tears from their eyes. The euphoria spilled out into the foyer where I could see Patricia smiling with relief (we all were!). She had captured these men's histories with dignity and empathy. The actors also were on a high, they had played the lines that night with unusual sensitivity. Patricia and I congratulated them all and we headed next door to the pub. As we entered, the Tunnel Rats cheered and insisted on buying beers for everyone involved. Pots were lined up along the bar and the accolades and stories flowed. It was a night I will never forget.

Nearly a year and half later, on the 5th August 2010, the HotHouse production of *The Berry Man* premiered at the Butter Factory in Wodonga. We all felt very proud of our work and believe we captured the 'spirit' and vivaciousness of *The Berry Man*.

Susie Dee
September 2011

Susie Dee directed the premiere production of *The Berry Man* for HotHouse Theatre. She has worked extensively in theatre as a performer and director both in Australia and overseas.

The Berry Man was first produced by HotHouse Theatre at the Butter Factory Theatre, Wodonga, on 5 August 2010, with the following cast:

ERIC	Greg Stone
MARJORIE	Maude Davey
ALEX	Tom Considine
JOEY	Ivan Donato

Director, Susie Dee
Designer, Darryl Cordell
Dramaturgical support, Campion Decent, Tom Healey
Lighting Designer, Gina Gascoigne
Sound Designer / Composer, Jethro Woodward

CHARACTERS

ERIC, a man in his 60s
MARJORIE, a woman aged 42
ALEX, a man in his 60s
JOEY, a 21-year-old man

SETTING

It is a rural setting. A great sense of space. Two farmhouses are represented simply by two verandahs or platforms with steps and balustrades and flywire doors.

MUSIC

Much of the play should be scored. This is not a play for sound effects or atmospherics. There is space for music.

SCENE ONE

ERIC *stands motionless in the middle of a newly hoed paddock. A hessian bag full of potatoes sits beside him. A mattock leans against the bag. He holds a potato the size of a small skull in his hand. He stares at it for a long time.*

MARJORIE *watches* ERIC *from some distance.*

MARJORIE: Look at you with your flannelette shirt and your big heavy boots, with your Hard Yakkas. Look at you with your mattock and your bag of spuds, your soil all tilled waiting to be sewn. If I held your hand I'd feel blisters along the pads of your palm. I bet they're hurting. And the splinters; the handle of your mattock needs sanding, anyone could tell you that. And what about your back? I can hear it groaning from here; it's saying, save me, I'm about to break, about to snap. It's not used to bending and lugging, it's too old for that. What are you doing to yourself? You're no farmer; you're no man of the land, no leather-skinned man. There's nothing you're going to grow. You're a holidaying man, doing something different for a while, experimenting with your lifestyle. You don't fool me, in a year you'll be gone. I'll drive down the road and there will be a 'For Sale' sign. [*She takes a step towards* ERIC.] Hello, Eric. Eric! [*She moves closer.*] What are you doing?

    ERIC *barely moves.*

ERIC: I don't like being snuck up on.
MARJORIE: I didn't exactly sneak up on you, Eric. I called.
ERIC: I didn't hear you.
MARJORIE: Must have been deep in thought. [*Pause.*] What are you doing, Eric?
ERIC: Planting spuds.
MARJORIE: Have you been here all day?
ERIC: What can I do for you, Marjorie?
MARJORIE: You haven't planted one.
ERIC: How can I help you?
MARJORIE: Not one potato.

ERIC: You my minder?
MARJORIE: Have you been standing here with that spud in your hand all day?
ERIC: You here to oversee me?
MARJORIE: They've got to go in the ground, you know.
ERIC: Piss off, Marjorie.
MARJORIE: Piss off?
ERIC: Yeah, piss off, that's what I said.
MARJORIE: That's real neighbourly, Eric.
ERIC: I don't need you coming over here to tell me how to farm my land.
MARJORIE: Your uncle never intended for you to work the farm.
ERIC: How would you know what he intended?
MARJORIE: Because he bloody well told me. He thought you'd sell.
ERIC: Is there something you want?
MARJORIE: Yes, there is.
ERIC: What do you want?
MARJORIE: I want you to get your bloody heifer out of my back paddock, that's what I want.

    ERIC *smiles*.

It's not funny, Eric. She's bent the pickets again.
ERIC: Genevieve likes the company of your sheep.
MARJORIE: She's pulled down the fence and I want it fixed.
ERIC: She's lonely.
MARJORIE: Get her mated.
ERIC: I'm not doing that.
MARJORIE: You know you have to calf her before you can milk her, don't you?
ERIC: She wouldn't want that.
MARJORIE: What?
ERIC: She doesn't need that.
MARJORIE: That's exactly what she needs.
ERIC: Genevieve's happy the way she is.
MARJORIE: Oh, for God's sake.
ERIC: I don't want her in calf.
MARJORIE: That's what she's for.
ERIC: No, she's here because I like her.

MARJORIE: She's an animal, Eric.
ERIC: I don't want to milk her.
MARJORIE: She's a cow.

> ERIC *smiles wryly.*

ERIC: She's the most gorgeous thing on Earth.

> MARJORIE *turns and walks away.*

MARJORIE: Get her out of my paddock.
ERIC: [*calling*] I've fallen head over heels for her.
MARJORIE: And fix the fence.
ERIC: She's the love of my life!

> MARJORIE *exits.*

SCENE TWO

A flywire door slams. ERIC *steps onto the verandah. Something in the dark has called him out.*

ERIC: I wondered how long it'd take for you to find me. I was beginning to think maybe you never would. I guess you've come to stay. You'll have to get used to me. I'm a new man, as they say. I don't drink anymore, and I've given up the choof. I'm as clean-cut as they come. No more drunken songs, no more songs at all. You might find me dull company. How are we going to be? Not much to distract us. Just you and me. Might get a bit intense, do you think? Who knows, perhaps we'll find some peace sitting on the verandah here, looking up at the sky. The skies are different here. They're enormous, overwhelming things. They demand silence. How will we go in the quiet with only the sounds of birds and the song of cicadas and the occasional toll of Genevieve's bell? [*He waits.*] I didn't leave you on purpose, Joey. I watch the road every day expecting to see you walking along it. As if I could lose you. You're stitched on.

> JOEY *finally steps into the light.*

JOEY: I did think that you'd done a runner, as a matter of fact.
ERIC: No chance of that.
JOEY: Thought you might have grown tired of me.
ERIC: Never.

JOEY: Might have found me a bit much.
ERIC: No.
JOEY: Might have wanted to wash your hands of me.
ERIC: Couldn't do that.
JOEY: Give me the boot.
ERIC: No way.
JOEY: No?
ERIC: No.
JOEY: Did you miss me?
ERIC: Terribly.
JOEY: Terribly?
ERIC: Like a pain in / the backside.
JOEY: / The backside. I don't believe you; I reckon you missed me more than that.
ERIC: I reckon you're right.
JOEY: You're right about the sky. It's bloody huge.
ERIC: It's daunting.

> JOEY *opens up his arms to the sky.*

JOEY: Could dive into it.
ERIC: You'll bloody drown. Come inside before I lose you again.

> JOEY *feigns fright. He runs up the stairs to the verandah.*

JOEY: I'm in.

> *He gives* ERIC *a quick kiss as he passes him and enters the house.* ERIC *follows him inside and the flywire door slams shut.*

SCENE THREE

MARJORIE *is out the flywire door and onto the verandah in a rush.*

MARJORIE: I wondered how long it would take for you to come. I heard your car. I know it's yours because it runs to a tune that misses a beat. I listen for it all the time. I heard your tyres when they rattled over the cattle grid and when they dug into the gravel as you took the curve. I heard you slam your door. Who'd have thought there was a difference in the sound of the slam of a car door? I heard your feet on the dirt. I heard you stop and knew you were grinding your cigarette out. I hear you all the time. I hear you when I lay in bed. I hear you when I'm at the sink running water for the dishes. I hear your feet on the verandah boards. And I come running. I run, brimming over with excitement, grinning with happiness because you've come, you've come back home. I've rehearsed my lines hundreds of times. I say, as if I could lose you. You're stitched on. [*Pause.*] Are you coming, Bob? Are you?

She waits expectantly but Bob does not appear. Her sadness is palpable.

I'm running out of time.

Silence.

SCENE FOUR

ERIC *and* JOEY *stand in the middle of a paddock.* ERIC *holds a pot plant in his hand. He stares at it for a long time.*

JOEY: I love jam.
ERIC: I know you do.
JOEY: Spread on thick white bread.
ERIC: The quicker we get these buggers tucked in the better.
JOEY: I can eat strawberry jam straight from the tin.
ERIC: It'll take a while before they'll bear fruit.
JOEY: And I love pies. Loganberry pie. Mulberry pie.
ERIC: They'll take off once they're in.
JOEY: And fresh berries, the way they stain your fingers when you pick them.
ERIC: Get the berries setting by spring.
JOEY: And how the juice spills over and runs down your chin.
ERIC: Got thousands of them. All types. Some I've never heard of.
JOEY: Such sweet things, berries.
ERIC: I'll need a hand planting them.
JOEY: Nothing but pleasure in them.
ERIC: I can't do it without you.
JOEY: I love them.

    ERIC *places the pot on the ground.*

ERIC: What do you think, Joe, a little dance to wish them well? A pagan kind of jig to protect them from the elements and the roos.

> *He dances with his knees up high for a few moments, but long enough to see him give in to the ridiculous.* JOEY *is greatly amused.*

My body's lost its elegance. It's got no grace, lost it a long time ago. I'm an insult to the fine elements which make things grow. What about you, Joey?

JOEY: What?

ERIC: Give us a dance.

JOEY: No chance.

ERIC: You could make this seedling burst through its pot and grab into the hard soil and root there and in moments spread its limbs, shoot leaves, form buds, flower and fruit, so that by the time I bent down I could pick a ripe blueberry here and put it in my mouth.

JOEY: You reckon?

ERIC: The gods would listen to your fine young body.

JOEY: No, they wouldn't. Would they?

ERIC: They'd be in awe of your beauty.

JOEY: Get out.

ERIC: They'd reward your goodness. They'd work overtime for you.

> JOEY *basks in the flattery.*

They'd give life to us all in thanks for a dance from such a beautiful boy.

> JOEY *dances wildly.*

The dance of the Berry Man.

SCENE FIVE

MARJORIE *is motionless in the dark in the middle of a paddock. She's dressed in a skimpy skirt and a sparkling top. Her hair is decorated with a sprig of jasmine. She carries a bottle of wine.*

MARJORIE: Eric. Eric. Eric!

> *The flywire door opens and a dishevelled* ERIC *stands on the verandah.*

ERIC: What's going on out there?

MARJORIE: Eric, it's me, Marjorie.
ERIC: What are you doing here, Marjorie?
MARJORIE: I was thinking about you, Eric, I was thinking that it's lonely here sometimes and basically you're a city man and you must be feeling like a bit of company every now and then and I'm only a few paddocks away and we should be friends. We should get to know each other better. It's silly how we've got. We've started off on the wrong foot and we should start again. We should spend a bit of time with each other, we should talk more, and go for a walk now and then, and share a meal and a glass of wine. And look, that's what I've brought. Get some glasses, Eric, and I'll pour us some wine.
ERIC: It's the middle of the night.
MARJORIE: I know, I know, but I thought, what the hell, I'm over there and you're here and who'd know? We can do what we like. It's the joy of living in isolation. Nobody knows what we get up to out here. We could drive the tractor without any clothes on; we could be part of a cult and whoop at the moon; we could be having a relationship with a cow. Who'd know?
ERIC: Go home, Marjorie.

She awkwardly turns in a circle.

MARJORIE: Do you think I brush up okay? Do you think that I look nice? Eric? What do you think?
ERIC: What the hell?
MARJORIE: Do you think the sprig of jasmine's a nice touch?
ERIC: It's late, Marjorie, go to bed.
MARJORIE: I don't think I can make it back. How about I come in and stay the night?
ERIC: You're drunk.
MARJORIE: Don't be like that, Eric.
ERIC: You're pissed, Marjorie.
MARJORIE: I've had a couple. For courage.
ERIC: I'm taking you home.
MARJORIE: Wouldn't it be lovely to spend some time together?
ERIC: Actually, Marjorie, no.
MARJORIE: For us to hang out a bit?
ERIC: What are you talking about?
MARJORIE: Getting together more.

ERIC: I'm not interested in having a relationship with you, Marjorie.
MARJORIE: How do you know?
ERIC: I'm not interested in having a relationship with anybody.
MARJORIE: I'm not talking about marriage or anything like that.
ERIC: I'm taking you home.
MARJORIE: Have you ever heard of having a bit of fun, Eric?
ERIC: What's brought this on?
MARJORIE: I've got needs like anybody else, you know.

> ERIC, *boots pulled on, comes down and takes* MARJORIE *by the arm.*

What's wrong with a bit of loving every now and then?
ERIC: You're going home.
MARJORIE: Jesus Christ, don't you know a good offer when you get one?
ERIC: I'm not interested.
MARJORIE: Why not?
ERIC: Come on, before you embarrass yourself.
MARJORIE: All I'm talking about is sex.
ERIC: I don't want to have sex with you.
MARJORIE: Don't be so old-fashioned, Eric. Women are allowed to ask for sex.
ERIC: I'm not interested in having sex with you.
MARJORIE: Don't be afraid.
ERIC: I'm not interested in you, Marjorie.
MARJORIE: It's your prostate.
ERIC: No.
MARJORIE: [*dawning on her*] Is there something wrong with me?
ERIC: Nothing's wrong with you, Marjorie.
MARJORIE: Close your eyes if you don't like the look of me. I don't care.
ERIC: You don't want to have sex with me.
MARJORIE: I find you very attractive, Eric, I forgot to say that.
ERIC: You don't even like me.
MARJORIE: We can have sex without liking each other. We can have sex just for the pleasure of it. Remember pleasure?
ERIC: Get going, Marjorie.
MARJORIE: What's a woman meant to do? I've tried to be nice. I've tried the subtle approach. Just have sex with me, for God's sake.

ERIC: You're going home.

She tries to kiss him.

MARJORIE: Let's just start again with a lovely little kiss.

He grabs her by the arm.

ERIC: Here we go.

She shrugs him off.

MARJORIE: I'll make my own way back, thank you very much. You're useless, Eric, do you know that?

ERIC *retreats inside.*

MARJORIE *remains looking at* ERIC*'s door.*

Eric. Eric. Eric!

ERIC *reappears.*

ERIC: Why are you still here, Marjorie?
MARJORIE: Have you got kids, Eric?
ERIC: No.
MARJORIE: Do you ever think you might have one?
ERIC: No.
MARJORIE: Never thought how nice that might be?
ERIC: Never thought about it.
MARJORIE: Never imagine yourself with a child, holding one, talking to one, playing with one?
ERIC: I decided a long time ago I wasn't interested in children.
MARJORIE: Surely you've thought about it at least once.
ERIC: I don't think there's much future for them.
MARJORIE: Oh.

Once again ERIC *retreats inside.*

Eric!

A very irritable ERIC *comes back out to the verandah.*

ERIC: Listen Marjorie…
MARJORIE: Eric, I'm forty-two.

Silence.

I want a baby.

ERIC: I don't know what to say to you.

MARJORIE: I want a baby and I don't have a husband or partner or even a boyfriend and I haven't got a lot of time and I think if I don't do something about it soon, very soon, it will be too late and my heart will break, so I thought, I wondered, if you would consider being the child's father. I think it's a wonderful idea because you're here and I'm over there and the child could come visit sometimes and you could visit too and he or she would know you and it would be such a convenient arrangement which could suit both me and you.

ERIC: No.

MARJORIE: No?

ERIC: I told you, I don't want a kid.

MARJORIE: We don't have to have sex. I can come over and collect your sperm and—

ERIC: Jesus, Marjorie, forget it.

MARJORIE: All I'm saying is if it's the sex, don't worry about it, I don't want to have sex with you either.

ERIC: What you're talking about sounds unnatural.

MARJORIE: Oh, Eric, lesbians do it all the time. It's perfectly normal.

ERIC: I'm not your man.

MARJORIE: You'd be working in the barn or mending a fence or on the tractor and some kid would wander over.

ERIC: I don't want to keep telling you the answer's no.

MARJORIE: Just a lovely sweet kid who's funny and curious and talks a bit.

ERIC: For a start, you know nothing about me.

MARJORIE: That's true. I don't.

ERIC: That's not very smart.

MARJORIE: Is there something wrong with you?

ERIC: There's got to be other men you can ask.

MARJORIE: I'm asking you.

ERIC: I'm the wrong man.

MARJORIE: Why's that?

ERIC: You'll meet someone, you'll fall in love and marry and start a family.

MARJORIE: I've run out of time for that.

ERIC: I'm not your man.

MARJORIE: Would you think about it?
ERIC: I don't need to.
MARJORIE: Take a little time to consider it, a day or two.
ERIC: Nothing will change my mind.
MARJORIE: Why not? Why can't you?
ERIC: It's too much.
MARJORIE: Too much?
ERIC: It is.
MARJORIE: It's too much to give me a baby?
ERIC: I think you should go home.
MARJORIE: A baby, that's all I want.
ERIC: Go home.
MARJORIE: That's all, Eric. That's it.
ERIC: Be reasonable.
MARJORIE: I've been reasonable all my life, so fair that I've been unfair to myself. Although it seems I'm asking a lot from you, I'm actually not.
ERIC: Go home, Marjorie.
MARJORIE: What's it to you? I mean it, what's it to you? Why do you care? In the scheme of things, what's it matter to you? I'll move away. Sell up and move so far away you wouldn't find us. You could forget all about it. It would be as if it never happened.
ERIC: Just go.
MARJORIE: Answer me and then I'll go. What's it to you?

Silence.

ERIC: It would turn out wrong.
MARJORIE: The situation, do you mean? Or the baby? Do you mean the baby?
ERIC: It would turn out wrong.

ERIC retreats inside.

MARJORIE walks away and suddenly stops. She returns.

MARJORIE: Eric!

ERIC opens the flywire door.

Fuck you, Eric, fuck you.

SCENE SIX

JOEY *and* ERIC *are in a paddock. The bag of potatoes sits full between them.* ERIC *has a mattock in his hands.*

JOEY: I like it here.
ERIC: Me too.
JOEY: I like it here a lot.
ERIC: Me too.
JOEY: Just me and you.
ERIC: Just me and you.
JOEY: It's peaceful.
ERIC: Quiet.
JOEY: Nothing here to sneak up on you.
ERIC: It's beautiful.
JOEY: We could stay here forever.
ERIC: Got nowhere else to go.
JOEY: Don't need much.
ERIC: Not much.
JOEY: Don't need anyone.
ERIC: Not at all.
JOEY: We've got each other.
ERIC: That's right.
JOEY: We could be self-sufficient.
ERIC: Get a vegie patch.
JOEY: And some chooks.
ERIC: Get them berries planted out.
JOEY: Fresh eggs every day.
ERIC: Get them into the ground.
JOEY: Have everything we want. Right here. Just you and me. Just you and me and Genevieve, in our own paradise.
ERIC: That'd be nice.
JOEY: A haven. A place no-one can get at us. Safe.
ERIC: As houses.
JOEY: I haven't felt happy like this in years. I'm happy. Are you?
ERIC: I'm happy.
JOEY: I love you. You know that, don't you?
ERIC: I love you too.

JOEY: You'll look after me, won't you?
ERIC: I'll do my best.
JOEY: No. You'll look after me, won't you?
ERIC: I will.
JOEY: You won't let anything happen to me. [*Pause.*] You won't let anything happen to me?
ERIC: No.
JOEY: It's going to be good.
ERIC: I reckon.
JOEY: Promise me.
ERIC: I promise.

SCENE SEVEN

ALEX *enters. He carries a slab of beer on one shoulder and a duffel bag on the other. He stops at the foot of the steps to Eric's verandah.*

ALEX: Is anyone home? Hey, there. Hello! [*He looks about, taking in the surrounds.*] Fucking fantastic.

    ERIC *comes quietly to the banister.*

ERIC: What can I do for you?

    ALEX *is overwhelmed at the sight of* ERIC.

ALEX: Have a look at you. Jesus Christ, it's taken me a while but I've found you. Eric, how are you, mate? [*Indicating the slab of beer*] I've come well-supplied, don't you worry about that. I've got another two slabs in the car. And I've brought some wine, a case of it in fact. Six reds and six whites because I wasn't sure what to get your wife. Going to give me a hand with this or what?

    He indicates the slab and ERIC *descends the stairs and automatically takes it. They hold each other's gaze for a moment.*

It's good to see you, Eric. I'd almost given up looking for you. I'll leave the rest in the car for the time being. I've got a box of food but mostly tinned stuff. [*Indicating his duffel bag*] Where will I park this thing? Don't go to any trouble. I'll bunk down anywhere. I'm used to doing it rough. I can tell you a story or two about the places I've slept in that would stand your hair on end.

> ERIC *puts the slab on the verandah. He turns and stares at* ALEX *intently. He begins to recognise him.*

ERIC: Alex. Alex Fisher. Fish. It's Fish.

> ALEX *scoops* ERIC *into his arms and hugs him tight. A dumbfounded* ERIC *does not respond.*

ALEX: That's right, mate, the Fish has found you at last.

> *For a moment too long,* ALEX *continues to hug* ERIC, *and then suddenly he drops his arms.*

I was looking in the wrong places. I didn't think country, not once. I didn't imagine you on a farm. I never thought of it.

ERIC: I've only been here a short time.

ALEX: Eric, a farmer, didn't cross my mind.

ERIC: I'm starting out.

ALEX: Tell me what you want done and I'll be into it. There must be a lot to do. Like to earn my keep while I'm here.

> *Pause.*

ERIC: Sure.

ALEX: You're a hard man to find, Eric. I didn't know whether you were dead or alive. I thought you must be still kicking because I never found you in the death notices. There's a few who have passed on. You know Macca's gone? And Elliot. Burton. Goldstein. Shit! Listen to me. I haven't even got in the door and I'm spewing out lists of the dead. I see Weathers regularly. He's fine. And Lawson. I've seen Pills and Jacko, but not for a while. I saw Straps but he could only have one drink before he had to catch a bus up North. That was ten years ago. Daniels, Lover Boy Anderson, Smiley and Bill C, I see them. I see Scottie every now and then. Milo and Johnny B, we keep in touch. I stayed with Bluey and his wife last year for a month or two. They've got a nice little unit back of the Gold Coast. [*Pause. He checks* ERIC *out.*] I nearly had you a few years ago. Pills had seen you come out of a boarding house in North Melbourne. He said he tried to speak to you but you didn't hear him and he lost you when you ran for a tram. I figured you might have lived there and took a punt and rang. Your landlady said I'd just missed you. You'd left the state she said, had gone only a day or two.

ERIC: That was twenty years ago.
ALEX: I thought you might turn up at the march. I looked out for you. We all did. Most of our lot were there. Like you, a couple had made themselves scarce and were hard to find. I'd looked for Dog for years. He came. But not you.
ERIC: No.
ALEX: It was fucking amazing. It was the march we never had. You should've come. [*Pause.*] I thought I might never see you again. I thought perhaps you were so far lost you could never be found.
ERIC: How did you find me?
ALEX: I read in the obituaries about the death of Albert Hornet and thought I might as well check it out. I didn't have any other leads and thought perhaps this Albert might be related to you. I found out he'd left this property to his nephew. So here I am.
ERIC: You didn't know I'd be here.
ALEX: Is your wife home? Your kids I guess would have gone by now.
ERIC: There's no wife. No kids.
ALEX: No wife and kids? I thought you would have been hitched up for sure. I always imagined you a family man.
ERIC: Not me.
ALEX: That surprises me.
ERIC: Why?
ALEX: I've been thinking about you for such a long time, I'd imagined you with your wife, your family. It's the picture I had of you in my mind.
ERIC: What are you doing here?
ALEX: What?
ERIC: What do you want?
ALEX: I'm visiting you, man. I've come to see you.
ERIC: It's been forty years.
ALEX: I know it. It's taken me this long.
ERIC: I don't get it.
ALEX: Had to know how you were getting on.
ERIC: Right.
ALEX: I thought you'd be pleased.
ERIC: It's forty years.
ALEX: Christ, Eric. I thought you'd be glad to see me.

Pause.

ERIC: I am.

ALEX: I knew you would be. There's a lot of filling-in to do. It's going to take some time. You here on your own?

ERIC: That's right.

ALEX: Got to tell you how the guys are getting on. Some stories are as miserable as hell. You'd expect that but there are lots of guys doing well, real well. And I want to know what's going on with you. [*Pause.*] Shit, it's good to be here. It's amazing, really. Honestly, I didn't know how much longer I could keep going. But I found you. I fucking found you.

He smiles at ERIC *and then picks up his duffel bag and goes inside.*

SCENE EIGHT

MARJORIE *returns to Eric's place.*

The silhouette of a man can be seen in the shadows.

MARJORIE: I've come back. I can't let it go just like that. I feel raw. I'm opened up, I've spilled my guts, and now I don't know how to tidy it all away. I feel too tender, too sore. I know I'm harassing you but I want you to reconsider for my sake. I've never done this before. I'm not the begging kind, I'm really not. I look like a nut. I am a nut, but what can I do? All the doors are shut and you're…

ALEX *walks into the light.*

ALEX: Eric's not here at the moment.

MARJORIE *is embarrassed.*

MARJORIE: I'm sorry, I thought…

ALEX: He's down at the dam fixing the pump.

MARJORIE: I didn't know Eric had anyone here.

ALEX: He'll be back soon, I reckon.

MARJORIE: Could you let him know…?

ALEX: You need to talk to him.

MARJORIE: No. Actually, I'm done. I'm right.

ALEX: I can go get him if you like.

MARJORIE: No, it's not important.

ALEX: It'll only take me a minute.
MARJORIE: No, it's okay.
ALEX: I'll let him know you dropped in.
MARJORIE: No need. Thanks, really it's okay.
ALEX: I'm Fish. Alex Fisher. I'm an old friend of Eric's.
MARJORIE: I'm Marjorie. Marjorie Hayes. Eric's neighbour.
ALEX: Come up and wait for him if you like.
MARJORIE: No thanks, I'll get going.
ALEX: I'm sure he won't be long.
MARJORIE: No, don't worry. Goodbye.
ALEX: I'll see you round some time.
MARJORIE: Yes, right.
ALEX: I'm here for a while.
MARJORIE: That's nice.
ALEX: Eric and I have got a lot of catching up to do.
MARJORIE: Right.
ALEX: It's good to be here.
MARJORIE: I mustn't keep you.
ALEX: Don't worry about it.
MARJORIE: Well, nice to meet you.
ALEX: You too, Marjorie.
MARJORIE: Yes, well, goodbye.

SCENE NINE

ERIC *stands with a sledgehammer in his hand.*
JOEY *sits on his haunches and looks miserable.*

ERIC: It'll only be for a while.
JOEY: But why?
ERIC: A short time, that's all. And then he'll be gone.
JOEY: Why are you doing this?
ERIC: Joey, it's not so bad.

    JOEY *begins to cry.*

JOEY: I don't want to be on my own.
ERIC: There's no reason to feel sad.
JOEY: You said you'd look after me.

ERIC: It won't be long.

His crying escalates.

JOEY: You said you wouldn't leave me.
ERIC: You're being childish.
JOEY: I am a child.
ERIC: You're twenty-one.
JOEY: [*a mini tantrum*] That's fucking young!
ERIC: Jesus! It's old enough.
JOEY: How can you say that? You know it's not. It's too young.

JOEY weeps piteously.

ERIC: You've got to stop, Joey.
JOEY: Can't.
ERIC: There's nothing can be done.
JOEY: That's why I'm crying so hard.
ERIC: It won't turn things around.
JOEY: I'm crying because there's nothing else I can do.
ERIC: It's too much, Joe.
JOEY: I know.
ERIC: You've got to keep it down.
JOEY: I don't think I can.
ERIC: Listen to me, you've got to stop.
JOEY: I'm trying.
ERIC: Stop, Joey.
JOEY: I'm trying.
ERIC: Stop!

JOEY settles.

Be strong, Joe, just for a little while.
JOEY: You don't like my tears, do you?
ERIC: They wear me out.
JOEY: They irritate you.
ERIC: They rub my nerves raw, that's all.
JOEY: I can't help it.
ERIC: We all feel it, Joey. We feel it as much as you do.
JOEY: I show it.
ERIC: Too much.
JOEY: I'm weak.

ERIC: No.
JOEY: I am.
ERIC: You're good, that's what you are.
JOEY: Good for fucking nothing.
ERIC: After he's gone, we'll be fine.
JOEY: What's he doing here?
ERIC: I don't know what he wants, but he wants something.
JOEY: Tell him to fuck off.
ERIC: Can you wait a while? Lie low? Just for a while.
JOEY: I'll try.
ERIC: I don't want him to suspect you're here.
JOEY: Why?
ERIC: He's scratching around. If he finds you…
JOEY: What? What'll he do?
ERIC: I don't know.

SCENE TEN

ALEX *enters in a rush and* ERIC *hurriedly turns to meet him.*

JOEY *has disappeared.*

ALEX: Are you alright?
ERIC: I'm fine.
ALEX: I thought you were hurt.
ERIC: Nothing wrong with me.
ALEX: Are you sure?
ERIC: Yes, of course I am.
ALEX: I swear I heard someone crying.

    ERIC *lifts his arm and swivels around to indicate he's alone.*

ERIC: Maybe a parrot squawking.
ALEX: I fell asleep. [*Indicating the sledgehammer*] Here, give us a go.
ERIC: All done.
ALEX: Shit, how long have I been sleeping?
ERIC: I started here three hours ago.
ALEX: You should've woken me. I thought I'd lie down and close my eyes for ten minutes and then come up and help. I can't believe I slept for three hours. Three hours! Are you sure?
ERIC: About that.

ALEX: I never sleep that deep. I think it's being here, on your farm. I think it's to do with finding you. I don't know why but I feel now I can. And I'm not bothered by dreams. How do you sleep?

ERIC: What do you mean?

ALEX: Do you have trouble sleeping?

ERIC: No.

ALEX: Your sleep isn't broken?

ERIC: I sleep through.

ALEX: I thought I heard you. In the night.

ERIC: Possums.

ALEX: You have weird dreams?

ERIC: No.

ALEX: No nightmares?

ERIC: No, I don't. I don't dream; I don't dream at all.

ALEX: You don't dream?!

ERIC: What is this?

ALEX: You're the only man I know free from visitations.

ERIC: What are you talking about?

ALEX: Appleby pops up in most of my dreams. He lifts his head and bays at the moon. Daniels has Daks visit his dreams. Half the night is spent with Daks raving about bringing the government down. Bluey bumps into Brenton at the same time every night. He comes around the corner of his street and Brenton comes in the opposite direction and they collide. His wife knows exactly when, because Bluey wakes her. He calls out in glee when he sees that Brenton's alive. And of course there's—

ERIC: I don't know who you're talking about.

ALEX: I'm talking about the boys.

ERIC: I don't remember them. They've gone. They've gone a long time ago.

ALEX: Where have they gone?

ERIC: I've forgotten them.

ALEX: All of them?

ERIC: Yeah, all of them.

ALEX: Did you forget me?

ERIC: Yeah, I forgot you.

ALEX: In all these years you never once gave me a thought?

ERIC: That's right.
ALEX: Never wondered about any one of us?
ERIC: No, it's all gone, it's in the past.
ALEX: That's amazing, Eric. Truly amazing.
ERIC: It just is. Nothing amazing about it.
ALEX: How did you do it?
ERIC: What?
ALEX: How did you manage to forget everyone?
ERIC: I got on with my life, I guess. I moved on.
ALEX: You never think about Vietnam?
ERIC: Not really.
ALEX: It never enters your mind, like sneaks in?
ERIC: It was forty years ago, Alex. That's a long time.
ALEX: Amazing.
ERIC: Not really.
ALEX: Does anyone know you went to Vietnam, Eric?
ERIC: Why should they?
ALEX: You've never told anyone?
ERIC: No, I haven't.
ALEX: Never came up in conversation?
ERIC: No, it didn't.
ALEX: That's unbelievable.
ERIC: Do you think I'm lying?
ALEX: Are you?
ERIC: I'm not fucking lying. I've let it go. I've got on with my life. I've got better things to do.
ALEX: Good for you.

SCENE ELEVEN

ALEX *is outside Marjorie's house.* MARJORIE *excitedly bursts out onto the verandah.*

ALEX: Hello.

> MARJORIE *cannot disguise her disappointment when she sees its* ALEX.

MARJORIE: Oh.
ALEX: I'm sorry, I appear to have got myself lost.

MARJORIE: It's easy enough to do.
ALEX: I set off hours ago and can't for the life of me find my way back.
MARJORIE: I'll drive you.
ALEX: If you point me in the right direction I reckon I'll find my way.
MARJORIE: It's actually not that far.
ALEX: I was stupid. I took off after Eric but I lost him.
MARJORIE: Where was he going?
ALEX: I don't know. I often can't find him. Sometimes I think he's hiding from me.
MARJORIE: What's he do with himself?
ALEX: He's always doing something.
MARJORIE: How does he fill his days?
ALEX: He's out and about.
MARJORIE: I've seen him standing like a scarecrow in the middle of a paddock, not moving a muscle.
ALEX: Probably just thinking.
MARJORIE: There's a bag of spuds out there rotting while he's thinking.
ALEX: He's new to it, isn't he?
MARJORIE: What's he do all day?
ALEX: He's up and gone before I wake in the morning. Puts me to shame.
MARJORIE: Where to?
ALEX: Feeding the cattle or sheep or something.
MARJORIE: He sold off all the livestock. Genevieve's all he's got and she's mostly at my place.
ALEX: I don't know what he's doing.
MARJORIE: He shouldn't be here.
ALEX: Why's that?
MARJORIE: He can't grow anything.
ALEX: He'll learn.
MARJORIE: You got to know what you're doing.
ALEX: Can't be that difficult.
MARJORIE: You've got to have a feeling for it.
ALEX: He'll get it.
MARJORIE: He'll never get it.
ALEX: Give him a chance.
MARJORIE: He'll wreck it.
ALEX: No, he won't. I'll help him.

MARJORIE: Do you know anything about running a farm?
ALEX: I've never even set foot on a farm before. I've done hundreds of jobs, in factories, in warehouses, on the process line. Never seen the sunshine.
MARJORIE: It takes a particular kind of mind.
ALEX: Never put seed in the ground, never held soil in my hands.
MARJORIE: You're going to be a great help.
ALEX: I'm looking forward to it.
MARJORIE: To what?
ALEX: To helping Eric with whatever he's got planned.
MARJORIE: If he's got plans.
ALEX: He's not useless, you know. He's a good man. He's one you could depend on in Vietnam.
MARJORIE: In Vietnam?
ALEX: That's where Eric and I met. We were in the same platoon.
MARJORIE: You're Vietnam vets.
ALEX: Look out, you've got a couple of time bombs about to go off. Two fellows about to go stark raving mad. Something you might say or do, a sudden movement, might trigger us off. Look out. I'm telling you.
MARJORIE: I wasn't thinking that.

She was.

ALEX: You're probably surprised I'm not here with a can of beer in my hand.
MARJORIE: Of course I'm not.
ALEX: Or did you think I might be carrying my rifle?
MARJORIE: No, I did not.
ALEX: Don't worry, I haven't felt so in the present for a long time. I've never felt so alive. I've got energy to burn. I could cut wood, build sheds, dig holes, plant things. I've never grown anything in my life, but somehow I know whatever I touch will grow.

SCENE TWELVE

ALEX *stands in the middle of a paddock.*

ALEX: Who's there? [*He listens.*] Show yourself. [*He waits.*] I heard you. I heard your scuffling feet, heard your laughter, heard you breathe. Come on, come on out.

JOEY comes up behind him and covers his eyes.

Who's this? As if I don't know. I wondered if you'd turn up, like a bad penny, a bad smell.

He reels around and tries to grab JOEY, *but he's too fast for him.*

JOEY: Way too slow, old man.

ALEX: I'll give you 'old man'.

ALEX lunges at JOEY *and misses.*

JOEY: What if you did catch me? What then? What, you'd give me a beating? I don't think so.

ALEX: I'll kick your arse down the road. I'll see you gone.

JOEY: I'm not going anywhere.

ALEX: I'll see the last of you.

JOEY: You'll never get rid of me.

ALEX: We'll see about that.

JOEY: You don't seem to understand. Maybe it's your age. I'm here and I'm not budging.

ALEX: You don't seem to understand that I'm not putting up with you. You're a leech, a parasite.

JOEY: And you're stuck with me.

ALEX: I can wait. I'll find a time that's right when I can put an end to you.

JOEY: I'm the sweat from your pores, I'm the taste in your mouth, I'm in your very bones. There's nothing you can do. You can't wash me off, I don't unglue. Mate, you're saturated in me. There's no sending me away, no putting me on a bus or train, no see you later, come another day, I'm here to stay.

SCENE THIRTEEN

ALEX *holds a tray of potted plants.*

ERIC: What do you think you're doing with them?

ALEX: There are thousands of them behind the shed.

ERIC: Put them back where you found them.

ALEX: What are they?

ERIC: Berries.

ALEX: Berries?

ERIC: That's right.

ALEX: Berries.
ERIC: Anything wrong with that?
ALEX: What kind are they?
ERIC: You name it.
ALEX: I love raspberries. You got them?
ERIC: Got them.
ALEX: I haven't had them since I was a kid. What about blueberries?
ERIC: And them.
ALEX: They're meant to be good for memory.
ERIC: So I've heard.
ALEX: Why berries?
ERIC: People like them.
ALEX: Right.
ERIC: They remind people of good times.
ALEX: What are you going to do with them?
ERIC: Plant them.
ALEX: When?
ERIC: Not yet.
ALEX: When?
ERIC: In a while.
ALEX: They look ready to go now.
ERIC: In a while, I said.
ALEX: They're looking a bit tired.
ERIC: What would you know?
ALEX: Let me help you.
ERIC: No.
ALEX: Why don't I dig the holes?
ERIC: No.
ALEX: They're not going to make it.
ERIC: They're alright.
ALEX: They look sad.
ERIC: Too bad.
ALEX: Why not plant them now?
ERIC: Didn't you hear me?
ALEX: I'll do it.
ERIC: I said no.
ALEX: I'd like to.

ERIC: Don't touch them.
ALEX: Let me.
ERIC: For fuck's sake, let it go!
ALEX: Just tell me. Why not?
ERIC: Because they won't grow.

SCENE FOURTEEN

Night. ERIC *and* JOEY *sit together at the bottom of the steps of Eric's verandah. They keep their voices low.*

JOEY: What about a fireman? I could save someone. Carry a woman over my shoulder, down the ladder, away from the flames.
ERIC: A fireman's good.
JOEY: Or a car mechanic. I'd like to be able to fix things that don't go.
ERIC: A car mechanic's good.
JOEY: What about a butcher?
ERIC: Have you got the stomach for it?
JOEY: No. What about a plumber or electrician, or gravedigger? [*Excited by the idea*] A gravedigger, that's it! I'll bury the dead.
ERIC: Keep your voice down, Joey.

    JOEY *lowers his voice again.*

JOEY: How long are we going to keep this up?
ERIC: Not long now.
JOEY: Forever.
ERIC: Soon it'll stop.
JOEY: Are you ashamed of me?
ERIC: I'm not ashamed of you.
JOEY: I reckon you are. Why else would you be hiding me?
ERIC: I'm not ashamed of you, Joe.
JOEY: What about a carpenter? I like the smell of wood.
ERIC: Yes, a carpenter's good.
JOEY: I'd like to make things. I've never made a thing. I've been a shit-kicker all my life.
ERIC: What about a baker?
JOEY: I could be anything I want.
ERIC: You could be a doctor.

JOEY: Got to be smart for that.
ERIC: You're smart.
JOEY: I left school when I was fourteen.
ERIC: You could go back.
JOEY: To school? No thanks. I could be a house painter, or an ambulance driver, or a tram conductor.
ERIC: You could.
JOEY: I could.
ERIC: Why not?
JOEY: It's not likely.
ERIC: Why not?
JOEY: Don't think I've got much future.
ERIC: Why do you say that?
JOEY: Don't reckon I'm going to amount to anything much.
ERIC: Of course you are.
JOEY: Doesn't matter.
ERIC: Of course it matters.
JOEY: I reckon I always knew it.
ERIC: What?
JOEY: I wasn't going to make it.

SCENE FIFTEEN

MARJORIE *and* ALEX *drink wine on Eric's verandah.*

ALEX: Do you get lonely out here?
MARJORIE: No. Sometimes. You get used to it.
ALEX: I don't spend much time on my own.
MARJORIE: You've got to have lots to do, but even still it can creep up on you.
ALEX: I like being around people. I like the noise of them.
MARJORIE: I do too. I like to stand on the verandah and listen to the chug of the tractor from the back paddock. I like to hear the splintering of the kindling when the axe slices through. I like the rustle of a newspaper, the sighs coming from another room. I like the sound of the soft sleepy words that I hear as I close my eyes last thing at night. The sounds of those I miss the most.
ALEX: You've not always been out here alone, I see.

MARJORIE: I was married to Bob for twenty years.
ALEX: Not a bad innings.
MARJORIE: I expected it to be longer.
ALEX: He took off?
MARJORIE: With a woman half my age.
ALEX: That'd hurt.
MARJORIE: They've had two kids. With me he never wanted any.
ALEX: And that'd hurt.
MARJORIE: One of them pains you think will never go away. What about you?
ALEX: I've been married three times and none of them lasted more than a couple of years.
MARJORIE: Kids?
ALEX: Four. Three. One died.
MARJORIE: I'm sorry.
ALEX: I don't see them.
MARJORIE: How come?
ALEX: I was never home.
MARJORIE: Why not?
ALEX: I spend most of my time with the blokes I was with in 'Nam.
MARJORIE: That would've been hard on them.
ALEX: The rest of the time I'm scouring the country looking for the rest of my platoon.
MARJORIE: Why?
ALEX: Because they're the most important people in my life.
MARJORIE: More important than a wife?
ALEX: Afraid so.
MARJORIE: Or child?
ALEX: That's right.
MARJORIE: How come?
ALEX: Because they know everything there is to know about me.
MARJORIE: And you found them.
ALEX: Cracked and bruised, I found them.
MARJORIE: And you finally found Eric.
ALEX: Eric's the last, and yes, I finally found him.
MARJORIE: You found them all and now you know they're alright.
ALEX: All the scattered pieces are accounted for.

MARJORIE: There must be something satisfying about that.
ALEX: I achieved what I set out to do.
MARJORIE: What now?
ALEX: I don't know.
MARJORIE: You can move on.
ALEX: That's right.
MARJORIE: There's nothing to keep you.
ALEX: No.
MARJORIE: You can start life anew.
ALEX: I can.
MARJORIE: Maybe you'll settle down.
ALEX: Maybe I will.
MARJORIE: Maybe you'll find somewhere and stay still.
ALEX: Maybe.
MARJORIE: You can do whatever you want.

Pause.

ALEX: Maybe.

ERIC *comes up the stairs, in from the night.*

Where've you been, mate?
MARJORIE: There's still some cheese and crackers on that plate.
ALEX: What can I pour you?
ERIC: Marjorie, it's time for you to go home.
MARJORIE: I beg your pardon?
ALEX: I invited Marjorie over for a drink.
ERIC: It's late.
ALEX: Join us.
ERIC: I've got a hard day tomorrow.
MARJORIE: Come on, Eric, I'll pour you a glass of wine.
ERIC: I want you gone.
ALEX: Oh, come on, mate…
ERIC: Do I need to remind you, Alex, that this is not your place?

Pause.

Marjorie, it's time you were on your way.
ALEX: This is not very hospitable, Eric.
ERIC: Now.

MARJORIE: For God's sake, I'm going.
ALEX: I'll walk you home.
ERIC: Marjorie can find her own way home.
ALEX: What?
ERIC: She'll be fine.
MARJORIE: I will, don't worry.
ALEX: I'm walking you home.
ERIC: She said she'd be fine.
ALEX: Eric! I'm walking Marjorie home.

They descend the steps.

ERIC: Don't be long!

ERIC *peers after them and finally retreats inside.*

SCENE SIXTEEN

The moon shines down on ALEX *and* MARJORIE *in the middle of a paddock. They burst into laughter.*

MARJORIE: Oh, my God.
ALEX: I feel about twelve years old…
MARJORIE: You better get back or he's going to tan your hide.
ALEX: Jesus Christ, I know, I know.
MARJORIE: 'Don't be long!'
ALEX: I think I must be standing on Eric's toes.
MARJORIE: How's that?
ALEX: He must fancy you.
MARJORIE: That is so far from the truth.
ALEX: He must.
MARJORIE: Eric does not fancy me.
ALEX: Why not? You're beautiful.
MARJORIE: Moonlight's playing havoc with your mind.
ALEX: You're beautiful.
MARJORIE: Oh, please.
ALEX: It's a pity I'm too old for you.
MARJORIE: I didn't notice.
ALEX: Thank God for the moonlight.
MARJORIE: Eric's fatherly outburst has made us young.

ALEX: Then I might find the courage to ask…
MARJORIE: What?
ALEX: It's gone.
MARJORIE: Ask me what?
ALEX: If I could kiss you.
MARJORIE: I don't see why not.

They kiss tenderly.

ALEX: I hadn't thought I'd ever kiss again and here I am kissing the sweetest mouth.
MARJORIE: Kiss it again.

They kiss.

ALEX: I'm warning you, I haven't made love for quite some time. I might disappoint you.
MARJORIE: You won't disappoint me.

Something is beginning to agitate ALEX.

ALEX: I can't go on.
MARJORIE: Go on.

ALEX *lifts his head to the skies and suddenly cries out in pain.*

Alex? What's wrong?

The pain continues.

Alex?

MARJORIE *retreats.*

SCENE SEVENTEEN

A jubilant JOEY *enters.*

JOEY: What's this?

ALEX *cannot answer.*

A man in misery. A man in tears. A man whose feelings have caught him unaware.

ALEX: You don't know the pain I feel.
JOEY: You dare ask me for sympathy?
ALEX: I'm asking you to understand.

JOEY: I've got none.
ALEX: You're cruel.
JOEY: I'm cruel! That's a good one. Have you forgotten what you've done?
ALEX: No, I haven't forgotten.
JOEY: It appears you have. Feeling sorry for yourself, feeling pain. You've got no right to complain.
ALEX: I've got every right.
JOEY: You gave that up.
ALEX: We were all in the same boat. Same age, same fears, we all wanted to get the hell out of there.
JOEY: And you did.
ALEX: I was as afraid as you, as confused as you, as overwhelmed.
JOEY: You came home,
ALEX: And as young.
JOEY: You came home.
ALEX: I was twenty-one.

SCENE EIGHTEEN

ALEX *raves.*

ALEX: When I came home I expected to be a hero, to be an Anzac like my father and grandfather. I expected to be feted, to be clapped on the back, to be congratulated. I met a woman I'd known since I was a kid in the street and she spat in my face.

On the steps of his verandah, ERIC *lifts his head from his hands.*

The RSL clubs told me I was a disgrace. I felt frightened and confused and lonely for a former life and returned to an Australia that disowned me.

ERIC *retreats inside. Seamlessly,* ALEX *shifts his focus to* MARJORIE *who sits on her steps. Time has passed in a matter of a breath.* ALEX *talks on without missing a beat.*

When I came home I looked at the letters I'd sent my mum. Every page was covered in kisses. We were boys when we went and we came home swearing, drinking, whoring men. I caught up with friends and their hair was long and they'd been overseas travelling with girlfriends. They weren't grown-up. They weren't men and I was angry with them. I'd had something stolen from me and nobody wanted to report it. Nobody wanted to talk about where I'd been, what I'd done, how I'd fared; they wanted to pretend I'd never gone anywhere.

> ERIC *comes down his steps and* ALEX *walks in his footsteps.* MARJORIE *retreats inside.*

When we came home we were snuck in, split up and sent off. They said, that's it, piss off, go live a nice suburban life. For two years we'd been together, walking in each other's footsteps, signalling with our eyes, covering each other's moves, lying in bed at night hearing each other cry. We had no idea how to contact each other or whether we'd ever see each other again. We were scattered bits and I had to put us together again.

> *Once again* MARJORIE *takes the next shift from* ERIC.

I came home to a girl who I'd written hundreds of letters. I'd held onto her in the dark, stifling nights. I'd held onto her in the mud and the slime. I'd held her hand when I walked through the maze of rubber trees and distorted light, where every shadow was someone about to take my life. I came home with pictures of our wedding already taken, our honeymoon already imagined. I knew her body, its shape, every dip and curve of her. I came home and she'd moved on. Gone.

MARJORIE: I'm sorry, Alex, it's late. I'm tired. I've got to go to bed.

ALEX: Yes, of course, Marjorie. I'm sorry; it's late, of course. [*He continues as if her interruption hadn't occurred.*] When we came home we learned that what you are now and will be until you're dead is a Vietnam War vet. That two years of our life crawled in and took up all the room. Nothing before and nothing after fit in.

MARJORIE: Goodnight, Alex.

> MARJORIE *exits to the slap of her flywire door and* ALEX *stops for a moment. He stares after her.*

ALEX: When I came home I feared only one thing. Tenderness. Any sign of it, the sweetest kiss, could bring me undone.

SCENE NINETEEN

Night. ERIC *is outside Marjorie's place.*

ERIC: Are you there, Marjorie?

    A sleepy, dishevelled MARJORIE *comes to the balustrade.*

MARJORIE: What is it?
ERIC: Is Alex with you?
MARJORIE: He's not here. [*Pause.*] He's not here.
ERIC: Don't fool with Alex, Marjorie.
MARJORIE: What do you mean by that?
ERIC: Don't muck him about.
MARJORIE: Alex is over sixty years old, Eric.
ERIC: He's vulnerable and you're…
MARJORIE: I'm what?
ERIC: You're after something and Alex doesn't need that.
MARJORIE: I'm 'after something'. You make it sound so crass. I'm after a baby. A baby, Eric, that's what I'm after.
ERIC: I don't want you to use him.
MARJORIE: It's none of your business.
ERIC: Alex is not the man to father your child.
MARJORIE: Who are you to decide?
ERIC: Leave him alone.
MARJORIE: It's got nothing to do with you.
ERIC: Don't bother him.
MARJORIE: I'll do what I like.
ERIC: I'm warning you, it wouldn't be wise.
MARJORIE: Alex is a grown man.
ERIC: Don't stuff him round.
MARJORIE: Leave me alone.
ERIC: He's not right.
MARJORIE: I noticed.
ERIC: Thank Christ.
MARJORIE: I like him.
ERIC: Marjorie, it wouldn't be kind.

    ERIC *exits.*

MARJORIE: I like him.

SCENE TWENTY

ALEX *follows* ERIC *out the door and down the steps.*

ALEX: I liked it when my birth date was called out. I liked it that something was expected of me. It was going to be an adventure; I didn't have to wait for life to begin any longer. I liked the idea of becoming a man. I barely knew my body and I liked it that it got stronger.

ERIC: Alex, give it a rest, would you?

ALEX: I liked us looking identical in our khakis, our spit-polished boots, our slouch hats. I looked in the mirror and thought, oh my God, I look like Dad.

ERIC: Something's got you going and you need to stop.

ALEX: We walked through the gates of the camp and we were instantly forgotten. Outside it was long hair and demonstrations and individualism and inside was compliance and obedience and discipline.

ERIC: You're wearing me out.

ALEX: Short back and sides took away our looks. Big ears became bigger, noses looked monstrous, chins were revealed which were almost non-existent.

ERIC: You're talking too much.

ALEX: Am I?

ERIC: You haven't stopped.

ALEX: I was looking for something to do with my life.

ERIC: Alex!

ALEX: I liked the idea that I was going to fight, to stop the commies from moving further south.

ERIC: Jesus!

ALEX: Someone in the paper wrote that you're better off killing a snake outside before it gets inside the house.

   ERIC *turns away from him.*

We were taught to fire a rifle, to use a bayonet, to throw grenades, to set mines, to see the enemy as nothing but a target, but it didn't occur to me that I would ever take a life

ERIC: Jesus Christ, can you shut up?! You've come unstuck. You're driving me nuts.

ALEX: The fear that ripped through my guts—

ERIC: That's enough, do you hear me? That's fucking enough!
ALEX: You didn't find it distressing, Eric?
ERIC: I find you distressing, Alex.
ALEX: You don't think about it?
ERIC: I've told you, I barely remember Vietnam.
ALEX: That's right, you've moved on.
ERIC: That's right, I have.
ALEX: You're fine.
ERIC: I am.
ALEX: The experience of Vietnam had no effect on you?
ERIC: That's right.
ALEX: You don't have any physical problems?
ERIC: I came back with both sets of arms and legs.
ALEX: No sudden sweats, no quickening of the breath, no heart palpitations, no rashes?
ERIC: None.
ALEX: I saw the rash down your front when you had your shirt off.
ERIC: That rash has got nothing to do with Vietnam.
ALEX: I recognised it because it's the same as mine.
ERIC: You're searching for signs that aren't there.
ALEX: What about your psyche?
ERIC: My what?
ALEX: You're inner being, your mental state.
ERIC: You asking me if I'm a nut case?
ALEX: Are you stressed?
ERIC: What are you talking about now?
ALEX: Post-traumatic stress.
ERIC: Alex, it was over forty years ago.
ALEX: Trauma doesn't just go.
ERIC: What's the fucking trauma? We spent a year in a war that long ago it doesn't matter.
ALEX: It doesn't just disappear.
ERIC: I don't need this shit. If all you want to do is talk about the agonies of Vietnam, I'm not your man.
ALEX: Do you feel much? About anything at all?
ERIC: I've just about had enough.
ALEX: I lost a child when she was four. She died and I could barely shed a tear.

ERIC: You've obviously done it tough, but I don't feel the same as you.
ALEX: You don't feel guilt?
ERIC: No, I fucking don't. You're not traumatised, Alex, you've just got nothing better to do with your life.
ALEX: There's not a man in our section who hasn't at some time fallen apart.
ERIC: We're in our sixties. Lots of men get to their sixties and discover life has disappointed them. Lots of them fall apart. Life is disappointing whether you've been to Vietnam or not.
ALEX: Not one who has not been traumatised by Vietnam.
ERIC: The whole fucking world is traumatised, Alex. You've been so consumed with yours, you haven't noticed.
ALEX: The whole fucking world, but not you.
ERIC: What do you want me to do? Do you want me to tell you that I lay awake terrified in the night? Do you think that I'm hiding something from you?
ALEX: Yeah, I do.

SCENE TWENTY-ONE

JOEY *rides* ERIC*'s back.*

JOEY: I'm slipping.
ERIC: I've got you.
JOEY: You're losing your grip.
ERIC: I've got you.
JOEY: I can feel it; you're going to let me go.
ERIC: I can't do this forever, Joe.
JOEY: You're strong.
ERIC: I'm old.
JOEY: You love me.
ERIC: You know I do.
JOEY: Don't let me go.
ERIC: I can't carry you.
JOEY: Too heavy for you?
ERIC: Yes.
JOEY: Too hard?
ERIC: Yes.

JOEY: You promised me.
ERIC: I know.
JOEY: You promised me.

SCENE TWENTY-TWO

MARJORIE, *once again dressed in skimpy skirt and sequinned top, hair up with a sprig of jasmine and make-up smudged after a night out, enters. She carries her shoes in her hand. She tiptoes past Eric's house.* ERIC *comes to the balustrade.*

ERIC: What do you think you're doing, Marjorie?
MARJORIE: Don't worry, I'm not after anything. You and your friend are safe. I drove my car into a ditch. So, excuse me, and I'm sorry to intrude, but I'm just passing through.
ERIC: Do you need some help?
MARJORIE: I can see fine in the moonlight.
ERIC: The car okay?
MARJORIE: It's just stuck. I was going too fast and braked too late.
ERIC: Tomorrow I'll bring the tractor up.
MARJORIE: Don't go to any trouble for me.
ERIC: I'll get the car and drive you home.
MARJORIE: I'm fine.
ERIC: Marjorie, it's alright.
MARJORIE: I wouldn't want you to think I'm using you. [*She looks at herself.*] Have a look at me, would you?
ERIC: Where've you been?
MARJORIE: I've been to the pub looking for a man. What do you think of that?
ERIC: It sounds a bit desperate.
MARJORIE: This is how desperate I am. I walk in and it's like I'm at primary school again. They're all lined up along the bar. There's Dougie Batten, Dill Lawson and Terry Angel, who immediately greets me with a kiss and takes a great chunk out of my lip. And Bob Slattery's there, holding the bar up, unbelievably pissed. I say to myself, you've come for a specific purpose, no point being choosy, just go for it. I talk to Dougie first and within a few minutes he tells me how he and a bloke from the abattoirs are having it off and he's

never been so in love in all his life. I try Dill next and the first thing he says is women are nothing but a bunch of cunts, so I thought to myself, move on. Terry Angel decides next to pinch me on the tit and so I give him a tap on the head with a bottle of Jack Daniel's which put him out to it. Bob Slattery's so pissed I knew he'd be next to useless and just when I think, this is stupid, give it a miss, Tom De Clario comes through the door. The perfect candidate. Tom's slept with every woman in the district. He's handsome and charming and everyone says he's good at sex. Perfect. He sees me and he tries to remember if he's had me and when he realises he hasn't he comes over and within minutes is covering me with kisses. I think this is it. We stagger out to the carpark still kissing. It's passionate, it's exciting, it's happening. He has me up against Dougie's ute and is struggling with his belt and finally drops the trousers of his suit and…

ERIC: And…?

MARJORIE: He tells me not to worry because he's had the snip.

ERIC: The snip?

MARJORIE: A vasectomy. I give up. I do. I truly give up

ERIC: Marjorie, I'll get you a glass of wine.

SCENE TWENTY-THREE

MARJORIE *sits between* ERIC *and* ALEX *on the steps of Eric's verandah. The men talk across her.*

ALEX: When we came home—

> Both ERIC *and* MARJORIE *gesture their frustration with* ALEX's *tirades.*

ERIC: Jesus Christ, don't start! No-one wants to know. It's a bore. Nobody in this country gives a fuck about war.

ALEX: Not the Vietnam War, that's for sure.

ERIC: No-one's interested.

ALEX: I'm talking to you.

ERIC: I don't want you to.

ALEX: I used to be silent like you.

ERIC: You're well and truly over that.

ALEX: What's the harm?

ERIC: I don't want to talk about the war.

ALEX: You can't tell me that nothing got to you.

ERIC: You think words are some kind of cure.

ALEX: Yes, I do.

ERIC: That talk takes away whatever is disturbing you.

ALEX: I think it's a way of getting things out.

ERIC: I think that some things deserve to be under lock and key.

ALEX: I think it's impossible to let things be.

ERIC: I've managed for over forty years.

ALEX: There's stuff we've done, we've seen.

ERIC: Do you want us to recount the horror stories of Vietnam? You first, then me, and then you again with something even more brutal, more horrific than the story before.

ALEX: There's stuff for us to talk about, I reckon.

ERIC: You want to talk, Alex. You can't stop.

ALEX: You think talking is for weak pricks. It's un-Australian. We don't do that, we don't spill our guts; we don't say we're sad or that we've been bad. We're tough; we take it on the chin. That's fucked.

ERIC: I've been in pubs sitting alongside diggers pissed out of their minds talking about their time, the only period in their life they ever felt intensely about anything. There they are dribbling on about how they gave up the best years of their lives, wiping a tear from their bloodshot eyes, lamenting the loss of a best friend…

ALEX: What are you afraid of?

ERIC: Nothing.

ALEX: Of feeling something?

ERIC: Oh, please.

ALEX: Of talking about Vietnam?

ERIC: Okay, here we go, I remember feeling a bit sad when I collected Wilson's scalp. It was hanging from a branch of a tree after he was blown to bits. And it upset me when we stood around Benson and he kept asking us to help him and we couldn't because it was with dying he needed helping. And it was stressful to be sent out on patrol rarely at full strength with some officer who was a dickhead and knowing that we were too tired, we were done in, over-stretched and half off our heads. It's all coming back to me now. Ears of Viet

Cong that were strung on a string around Abbott's neck, along with his dog tags and his crucifix. That even got into my dreams. A field of rice caches that were actually dead bodies writhing in maggots. That got into my dreams. On the way to R and R on a truck and Slats pulls out a grenade and drops it in the street blowing some poor bastards doing their shopping to smithereens. I can go on, if you like. Because you're right, there's nothing to it, it's a piece of cake talking like this. I could go on for hours.
ALEX: Whatever you like.
ERIC: Alex, it's obscene.
ALEX: I'm waiting.
ERIC: What for?
ALEX: To talk about Joey.

Silence.

MARJORIE: Who's Joey?
ERIC: Let's leave Joey be.
ALEX: Can't.
ERIC: Why not?
ALEX: Because I reckon it's going to save your life.
ERIC: I've finally got you pegged. You do the rounds. You wander across the country looking for your long-lost mates and uninvited you move in and take up all the space. You prattle on with your yearning for the old days. You talk so much we're in a daze. You talk and talk until you wear everyone out. I want you on your way.
ALEX: Eric…
ERIC: No. No more talking. I want you gone.

SCENE TWENTY-FOUR

ERIC *remains motionless in the middle of the paddock.*

ERIC: Jesus.

　　ALEX *enters, his duffel bag packed and slung over his shoulder.*
ALEX: What is it?

　　He moves closer. ERIC *gestures to him to stop.*

　What is it, Eric? What's wrong?

ERIC: Leave me alone.
ALEX: What's going on?
ERIC: Get going, Fish, will you? Just leave me.
ALEX: I'm not going anywhere.
ERIC: Piss off!
ALEX: What's going on?
ERIC: Would you go, would you just go!?
ALEX: No way, I'm not leaving you out here on your own.

> ERIC *lifts his head to the gods.*

Jesus Christ, what's going on?

> ERIC *slowly drops his head to look down at his feet.* ALEX *follows his gaze and finally understands.*

It's nothing, Eric, I'm telling you, it's nothing at all.
ERIC: I heard it.
ALEX: It was a stick, just a stick snapping beneath your feet.
ERIC: I felt it.
ALEX: I promise you, it's your mind playing tricks.
ERIC: Fish, help me.
ALEX: Take my hand.
ERIC: I can't lift my foot.
ALEX: Believe me, take my hand.

> ERIC *laughs quietly.*

ERIC: This is fucking ridiculous, isn't it?

> ALEX *laughs too.*

ALEX: It is. Fucking ridiculous.

> ERIC *takes* ALEX' *outstretched hand. They hold the grip for some time.*

SCENE TWENTY-FIVE

ALEX *and* ERIC *wait.*
JOEY *emerges from the shadows.*
They do not look at JOEY.

ERIC: Can you see him?

ALEX: I can.

> JOEY *steps closer.*

ERIC: Three young lads on tour in Vietnam.
ALEX: It's exciting.
ERIC: An adventure of a lifetime.
ALEX: Never set foot on a plane before.
ERIC: One year is all.
ALEX: One year and we're done.
ERIC: Our first rec leave and we go to Vungers looking for girls.
ALEX: Never fucked a girl before.
ERIC: It's the first sign that Joey's not right.
ALEX: We set him up with a pretty girl about fourteen years old.
ERIC: He's resistant but we get him drinking and we're persistent.
ALEX: We think that Joey needs to fuck a whore.
ERIC: From then on he starts to withdraw.
ALEX: Becomes more and more distant.
ERIC: One year is all.
ALEX: And we'll be done.
ERIC: Out on patrol he can't be depended on.
ALEX: He never fires a single shot.
ERIC: He never killed anyone.
ALEX: But it makes no difference because he feels he pulls the trigger on every gun.
ERIC: One year.
ALEX: One year is all.
ERIC: Joey doesn't speak anymore.
ALEX: Back at the Dat we find him standing in the showers, a cake of soap in his hand.
ERIC: In the boozer, with all the yelling and singing and punching on, he's standing in a corner with a warm can of beer in his hand.
ALEX: Standing there, but gone somewhere.
ERIC: And there's something damning about his silence.
ALEX: But it's the crying that gets to everyone. The constant sobbing. At first it's only when he's in the cot.
ERIC: Then he's crying non-stop. It's like some kind of judgement on us.
ALEX: Then we start to hate him.

Pause.

ERIC: The end of the year's in sight.
ALEX: Two weeks is all.
ERIC: Thank Christ.
ALEX: Two weeks and our tour will end.
ERIC: And we'll be on a plane out of here.
ALEX: I see the calendar by my cot, the big day marked off.
ERIC: We've had enough.
ALEX: We're sick at heart.
ERIC: We're dulled down.
ALEX: Without spark, waiting for it all to come to an end.
ERIC: Two weeks and we'll be free.
ALEX: Flown back to our families.
ERIC: Two weeks. [*Pause.*] One last patrol. We're pushing our luck.
ALEX: I think, this is it, we're fucked.
ERIC: The gods are after a sacrifice.
ALEX: We lead out.
ERIC: Joey follows.
ALEX: He refuses to carry his gun.
ERIC: Leaves it on the track.
ALEX: Drops his backpack from his back.
ERIC: Walks along in a daze.
ALEX: I'm angry with him.
ERIC: Once again we're carrying him.
ALEX: Protecting him.
ERIC: Covering for him.
ALEX: I think, fuck you, after all we've done for you.
ERIC: There's no blood on your hands.
ALEX: No notches on your belt.
ERIC: You're clean.
ALEX: And we're the murdering bastards.
ERIC: You're the good boy.
ALEX: The boy with a conscience.
ERIC: The boy who still feels something.
ALEX: And we're heartless.
ERIC: Straps circles back.
ALEX: He signals to us that a group of Cong are heading our way.

ERIC: And we fall into positions for an ambush.
ALEX: We drop to the ground.
ERIC: Keep our heads down.
ALEX: Tuck ourselves into the dirt.
ERIC: And leave Joey standing empty-handed on the track.
ALEX: No-one tells him.
ERIC: No-one gives him a sign.
ALEX: It's as if we've made some secret pact.
ERIC: All of us of the same mind. [*Pause.*] We wait.
ALEX: We wait.
ERIC: Not long.
ALEX: And they come.
ERIC: He looks so young.
ALEX: Unsuspecting.
ERIC: Just a boy.
ALEX: He doesn't flinch.
ERIC: His body scatters into a thousand pieces it seems.
ALEX: And Joey's gone.
ERIC: Gone.

> JOEY *has disappeared in the darkness.*

SCENE TWENTY-SIX

ERIC, ALEX *and* MARJORIE *stand with a berry pot plant in each of their hands.*

ERIC: Last ones.
ALEX: Almost done.
MARJORIE: We've done well.
ERIC: They look good.
ALEX: Thousands of them.
MARJORIE: They'll take off now.
ERIC: Berry pies before long.
ALEX: I'll be your chief taster.
ERIC: Okay, here we go.

> ERIC *and* ALEX *bend to put the plants into the ground.* MARJORIE *remains standing. She groans.*

ALEX: You right?
MARJORIE: I think so.
ERIC: Sit down for a bit.
MARJORIE: I feel a bit sick. [*She takes a breath.*] I'm right.

She joins the others and they put the last three plants into the ground.

THE END

COPYING FOR EDUCATIONAL PURPOSES

The Australian *Copyright Act 1968* (Act) allows a maximum of one chapter or 10% of this book, whichever is the greater, to be copied by any educational institution for its educational purposes provided that that educational institution (or the body that administers it) has given a remuneration notice to Copyright Agency Limited (CAL) under the Act.

For details of the CAL licence for educational institutions contact CAL, Level 15/233 Castlereagh Street, Sydney, NSW, 2000; tel: within Australia 1800 066 844 toll free; outside Australia 61 2 9394 7600; fax: 61 2 9394 7601; email: info@copyright.com.au

COPYING FOR OTHER PURPOSES

Except as permitted under the Act, for example a fair dealing for the purposes of study, research, criticism or review, no part of this book may be reproduced, stored in a retrieval system, or transmitted in any form or by any means without prior written permission. All enquiries should be made to the publisher.

www.currency.com.au

Visit Currency Press' website now to:

- Buy your books online
- Browse through our full list of titles, from plays to screenplays, books on theatre, film and music, and more
- Choose a play for your school or amateur performance group by cast size and gender
- Obtain information about performance rights
- Find out about theatre productions and other performing arts news across Australia
- For students, read our study guides
- For teachers, access syllabus and other relevant information
- Sign up for our email newsletter

The performing arts publisher

www.ingramcontent.com/pod-product-compliance
Lightning Source LLC
Chambersburg PA
CBHW042130160426
43198CB00022B/2964